INTERNET FOR EDUCATORS

Second Edition

RANDALL JAMES RYDER
University of Wisconsin, Milwaukee

TOM HUGHES
Intuitive Systems
Waterford, WI

Merrill,
an imprint of Prentice Hall

Upper Saddle River, New Jersey   Columbus, Ohio

Library of Congress Cataloging-in-Publication Data

Ryder, Randall J.
    Internet for educators / Randall James Ryder, Tom Hughes, -- 2nd ed.
        p.   cm
    Includes bibliographical references and index.
    ISBN 0-13-699075-4 (pbk.)
    1. Education -- Computer network resources.   2. Internet (Computer
network) in education.   I. Hughes, Tom, 1950-   .   II. Title
LB1044.87.R93   1998
025.06'37--dc21   97-45603
                                                                                    CIP

Editor: Debra A. Stollenwerk
Production Editor: Louise N. Sette
Design Coordinator: Karrie M. Converse
Cover Designer: Brian Deep
Production Manager: Deidra M. Schwartz
Director of Marketing: Kevin Flanagan
Marketing Manager: Suzanne Stanton
Advertising/Marketing Coordinator: Julie Shough

This book was set by Carlisle Communications, Ltd., and was printed and bound by Courier/Kendallville, Inc. The cover was printed by Courier/Kendallville, Inc.

 © 1998 by Prentice-Hall, Inc.
Simon & Schuster/A Viacom Company
Upper Saddle River, New Jersey 07458

Printed in the United States of America

10 9 8 7 6 5 4 3 2 1

ISBN: 0-13-699075-4

Prentice-Hall International (UK) Limited, *London*
Prentice-Hall of Australia Pty. Limited, *Sydney*
Prentice-Hall of Canada, Inc., *Toronto*
Prentice-Hall Hispanoamericana, S. A., *Mexico*
Prentice-Hall of India Private Limited, *New Delhi*
Prentice-Hall of Japan, Inc., *Tokyo*
Simon & Schuster Asia Pte. Ltd., *Singapore*
Editora Prentice-Hall do Brasil, Ltda., *Rio de Janeiro*

For Sydney, the original NetDog.

CONTENTS

PREFACE

This is a book about the Internet and its applications to school settings. Its intended audience is preservice and inservice teachers who would like to begin to explore the functions of the Internet and its applications to classroom learning. Because of the special considerations and constraints presented in educational settings, we have approached the content of this book from the assumption that the integration of the Internet into the curriculum requires a particular approach to instruction. This approach has special implications to the teacher, the student, and the educational system.

Imagine a learning environment where learners construct knowledge as well as receive knowledge generated by others, an environment allowing the student to explore a subject or topic presented from sources spanning the globe. Imagine these sources providing students information in the form of text, graphics, audio, and video. Imagine the learner interacting directly with experts and peers throughout the world.

Welcome to the world of the Internet and the World Wide Web!

A generative model of instruction

It has been our experience that as educators become more familiar with the resources and tools of the Internet, they increasingly become aware of the need to acquire different forms of instruction. Frequently, their attention is drawn to generative forms of learning—learning characterized by learners who create authentic or real-life learning tasks, who elaborate on that task by exploring informational sources, and who represent new ideas or insights by reaching conclusions or producing a product. This product itself can be used to inform the student, but it can also be used as a means to represent and share the artifacts of the student's knowledge by transmitting that information by electronic mail or creating a permanent site on the Internet where others can view the learning products.

It is our position that successful development, implementation, and refinement of learning environments that apply some form of generative model of instruction as they use the resources of the Internet are based on commonly held tenets of effective learning. These tenets include the following:

Learning is active

Students are likely to learn best when they are manipulating, exploring, observing, using various sensory modalities, discussing, experimenting, or otherwise being truly involved in the process. In the context of the Internet, students would be encouraged to explore various sources, to generate questions, to seek answers to their own questions, or to solve problems by seeking information, guidance, and support from individuals or resources on the Internet. This form of learning is in contrast to passive learning where the learner is viewed as a sponge whose primary purpose is to memorize details, to listen but not inquire. Those who advocate passive forms of learning assume that by acquiring a lot of information, students will eventually be capable of making sense of the world by applying their wealth of information even though they may lack the tools to synthesize and apply that information.

Unfortunately, without the benefit of strategies that teach students *how* to apply this "inert" knowledge, few will likely be capable of constructing meaning without considerable assistance or frustration.

Learning is tailored to the individual

Because students learn in different ways, and they learn better when they can relate their personal experiences and perceptions to the learning task, learning on the Internet should allow students the opportunity to acquire information or approach a task in different ways, to generate their own artifacts of learning (essays, journals, videos, class presentations, information placed on the home page of an Internet site) in a manner that best characterizes their own style of learning. Assessing the learner then may take the form of providing feedback on any of these products, or it may involve acquiring feedback from students or teachers who examine and provide feedback on artifacts that are displayed on the Internet. Recognizing the students' individual contributions and their unique approaches to learning, the Internet provides a flexible and dynamic context where all students explore resources that best fit their cognitive style of learning.

Learning involves others

Cooperative efforts—students working together—tend to encourage active learning, allow students to entertain diverse points of view, and create a climate for mutual support and respect. The Internet extends cooperative learning arrangements beyond the walls of a classroom to involve students at a national or international level. Cooperative arrangements also minimize the effects of isolated learning that occur with many computer software applications.

Learning requires specialized strategies

Students are likely to learn better when they consciously apply certain strategies to the learning task that direct their thinking, that encourage them to monitor and evaluate their progress as they engage in the task, and that allow them to activate additional strategies or processes when things go wrong. Although learning certain amounts of facts, details, and fundamental information is important, it is also important for learners to develop strategies that permit them to know how to acquire knowledge.

Learning is contextualized

Learning is more relevant, reflects demands of the real world, and is likely to promote generalized strategies when it occurs in meaningful, authentic contexts. For example, students are much more likely to gain an understanding of life in Russia by participating in an e-mail project involving contact with various elements of that country than by just reading a page or two from a textbook. Unlike most instructional tools, the Internet has the potential to provide rich, multimedia contexts for learning.

Students can visit museums, tour the White House, view photographs from satellites, participate in global discussion groups, hear live transmissions from distant locations, and have actual face-to-face video conferences with individuals from various occupations and geographical locations.

We have attempted to apply these tenets to the writing of this book in several ways. First and foremost, we limit our discussion of instructional applications to those that acknowledge the preceding tenets. As with any new technology, there is the inevitable rush to make the new technology fit existing instructional paradigms. We are reluctant, for example, to acknowledge the value of an activity limited to directing students to the Bureau of the Census Internet site to record the population of the fifty states and the twenty largest cities.

Second, we advocate the position that when learning activities involve the Internet, the teacher will assume the role of a facilitator or coach in an effort to assist students to learn for themselves. As such, many of the activities we address are student directed, often involving cooperative learning arrangements that stretch beyond the confines of the classroom to include peers in various geographical locations. Naturally, this involves some risk taking on behalf of the teacher. The burden of providing information shifts from the teacher to the student's ability to access Internet resources. Finally, we have chosen to discuss the educational applications of the Internet from the position that the Net offers a rare opportunity to effect significant change in the way we teach and the way students learn. Accordingly, we have devoted an entire chapter to the procedures for setting up an Internet site for your school or classroom. Although your initial efforts in applying the various tools of the Internet will likely be devoted to navigating, locating, gathering, and disseminating information, we hope you will embrace the notion that you and your students will view the Internet as a vast storehouse of information and tools and as a medium for communicating and sharing your resources with your community and the world.

The organization of this book

This book contains four chapters. The first is an overview for individuals who are getting started on the Internet. It includes a section defining the Internet and its components, the topic of netiquette and objectionable materials, ways to connect to the Internet, and various types of software providing access to various components of the Internet. The second chapter discusses communicating and exploring for information on the Internet. This chapter presents an overview and instructional applications of e-mail, listservs, and Usenet newsgroups. The chapter concludes with a presentation on ways to receive files and how to locate information on the Internet. The third chapter presents ways to evaluate information on the Internet, instructional activities for the Internet, and strategies to assist students in filtering information to facilitate the construction of knowledge. The fourth and final chapter is designed to provide an overview on the use of HTML, an easy-to-learn programming language that can be used to design your own web site on the Internet.

Special features of this book

In an effort to create a book that is easy to understand, relevant to the needs of teachers, and that provides a user-friendly environment, we have added the following features:

- Chapter Overviews—Each chapter begins with a concept map and a brief written summary of the chapter's content.

- Screen Images—Interspersed throughout each chapter are screen images displaying actual content of the Internet and text and graphic images that we have downloaded from the Net.

- Highlighting the Language of the Internet—Throughout the text, vocabulary unique to the Internet (or what is referred to as N*etspeak*) occurs in boldface type. We have also included a glossary at the end of the book.

- Practice Exercises—At the end of each chapter is a section providing activities to engage in and apply various Internet tools and instructional strategies.

- Wide Margins and a Spiral Binding—To encourage you to make notes or comments on various subjects addressed in the text, we have allowed rather wide margins. It is our experience in teaching courses on the Internet that students will normally make various sorts of margin notes to draw their attention to information or to make annotated comments. And that spiral binding? Frankly, if you're like us, we have great difficulty in referring to specific pages of a book as we are working on our computers. We've tried weights, large cups of coffee, small plants, and a stuffed walleye. So we decided that a spiral bound text was in order.

A very cool supplement to this book: Our own Internet site for educators!

Visit our site at this World Wide Web address:

http://www.execpc.com/~hughes/

Acknowledgments

We would like to express our sincere thanks to a number of people who have assisted us in the preparation of this book. First, we would like to thank all the citizens of the Internet who have taken the time to provide us feedback on the content of this book, to provide us information on various applications of the Internet, and who have answered numerous technical questions. Without their dedication to their craft and their willingness to share their knowledge and resources, the writing of this book would have been a rather arduous task. Second, we would like to express our appreciation to the outstanding assistance and support we received from Debbie Stollenwerk, Penny Burleson, and Jeff Johnston at Prentice Hall. Thanks to their vision, their ability to assist us in advancing some novel approaches to create a book of this nature, and their professional manner, writing this book was an enjoyable experience. Finally, we would like to thank the following reviewers for their informed comments, their interest in creating a text that would serve the needs of educators, and their encouragement of our efforts: Lorana Jinkerson, Northern Michigan University; Thomas Smyth, University of South Carolina—Aiken; David Spillers, University of Arkansas at Little Rock; Neil Strudler, University of Nevada Las Vegas; and Bernard Ulozas, National University.

CHAPTER 1 — GETTING STARTED ON THE INTERNET

OVERVIEW

This chapter provides an introduction to the Internet (Figure 1) and explains:

- what the Internet is and what you can expect to find on it,

- potential misuses of the Internet,

- basic methods of getting on the Internet from either your home or school,

- Macintosh and Windows software for accessing the Internet, and

- how to construct an Intranet, a self-contained internal network, instead of using the Internet.

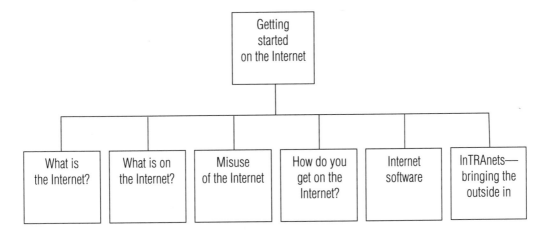

Figure 1: Chapter 1 concept map.

WHAT IS THE INTERNET?

In a small town nestled in the Rocky Mountains of New Mexico, Kaye Coletto is about to begin her day with thirty-two fifth-graders. As she enters her room, she turns on the master switch for six classroom computers connected to the school's network. Kaye quickly logs into her account to retrieve her e-mail and soon finds a message from a teacher in Mexico City whose fifth-grade class will be collaborating with Kaye's class on a science experiment examining the effects of air pollution. Over the last two weeks, the classes in New Mexico and Mexico City have been gathering climatic and pollution data to determine the effects of humidity, wind currents, barometric pressure, and temperature on various indices of pollution. Several students in the two classes engage in daily voice discussions on the Internet, transfer photos they have scanned, and exchange data they post on the World Wide Web.

Today will be the culminating effort of their investigation when their findings will be discussed class to class over a video link established on the Net. Also joining the video conference from Boulder, Colorado, will be a scientist working at the National Center for Atmospheric Research. Parents in the community will be observing the interactions as well over their office and home computers that have been dialed into the school's computer server. But all of these activities will not occur for several more hours.

For now Kaye must use the Internet to obtain a copy of a treaty from the Library of Congress, download some science software from NASA and a complete book from Project Gutenberg, place an order for classroom supplies with a vendor in Florida, then finally respond to various e-mail messages from parents.

Futuristic? No, just another day in the life of a classroom teacher applying today's technology.

In just over a few years, the Internet has emerged from near obscurity to become an information phenomenon. Connecting most of the world, the Internet truly is an international medium, as illustrated in Figure 2.

Created in 1969 by the United States Defense Department, the Internet (or ARPA*net* as it was then called) was designed to link a number of military sites together to form a research network. However, computer networks at that time were rudimentary and not very robust; that is, if one link or computer failed, the entire network might collapse. The military needed a "bombproof" network that could still function even if parts of it failed. In order to accomplish this, a computer on the ARPAnet had multiple connection paths to the other computers on the network so that even if one (or several) of these paths was not working, another one could be used (Figure 3).

This technical ability to "route around damage," or to select different paths, has implications for those attempting to censor information on the Internet. For example, in Figure 3, if for some

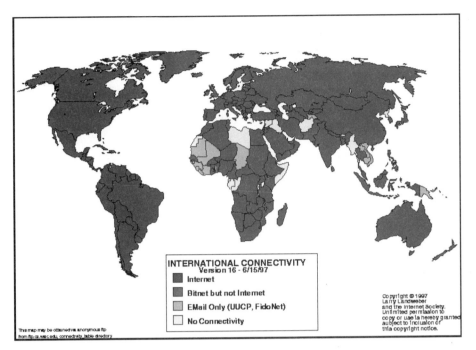

Figure 2: Countries connected to the Internet.

reason you didn't want your students who use Computer A to access Computer E, how would you prevent it? Since asking the owners of Computers B, C, and D to drop their connections to Computer E would be impractical, your only recourse would be to disconnect Computer A from the network. Again, not a very practical solution. However, there are ways to restrict a user's access to information on the Internet (see "Misuse of the Internet").

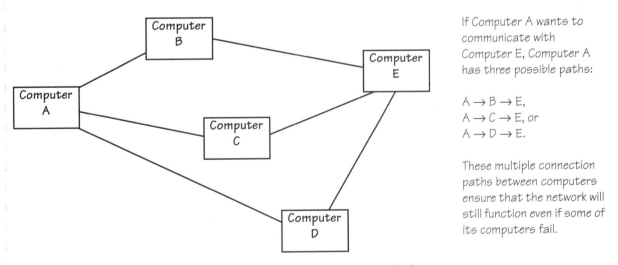

If Computer A wants to communicate with Computer E, Computer A has three possible paths:

A → B → E,
A → C → E, or
A → D → E.

These multiple connection paths between computers ensure that the network will still function even if some of its computers fail.

Figure 3: How computers communicate on the Internet.

In 1986 the National Science Foundation Network, or NSFNET, (http://nic.merit.edu/nsfnet/final.report/intro.html[1]) was created by the U.S. government as a noncommercial computer network and connected six nationally funded supercomputer sites at a speed of 56 **Kbps** (kilobits per second). As a result of increased use, this network speed was bumped up to what's known as "T1," which is 1.544 **Mbps** (megabits per second), in 1989. However, this merely served to accelerate Internet usage, and in 1991 the NSFNET began using "T3" service, which is 45 Mbps—a 2800% increase in just two years!

On April 30, 1995, most of the functions of the NSFNET were replaced by a number of commercial services such as MCInet and Sprintlink. Since then there has been a dramatic increase in the number of commercial WWW sites which offer every conceivable service and product. Even though this rapid growth has been coupled with improvements in the Internet's infrastructure, such as its bandwidth, delays and even network breakdowns are increasingly common.

The "mother-of-all-networks"

The Internet is a "network of networks" that connects computers across the world into one gigantic global communications system that allows all the computers on the Internet to share and exchange data. In computerspeak, the Internet is a wide area network (**WAN**) (Figure 4) composed of many local area networks (**LAN**s). A LAN is simply two or more computers wired together so that each can communicate and share information with the other. Think of a computer on a LAN like a house with telephone service. A WAN, therefore, is a network of networks.

Hypertext: the "web" of the Internet

Part of the reason for the Internet's exponential growth[2] is its increasing ease of use. Until very recently, navigating the Internet required knowledge of UNIX, a difficult computer language. This restricted access until **World Wide Web** (also called WWW, W3, or the Web) **browser** software such as Internet Explorer and Netscape became available. These WWW browsers resemble Microsoft's Windows and Apple's Macintosh in that they have graphical user interfaces with point-and-click interactions. The browsers are readily learned and use **hypertext** to provide a multimedia environment previously unavailable (Figure 5).

Hypertext is largely responsible for making the Internet an easier place to visit. Hypertext links information together, and it is the connecting web of the World Wide Web (Figure 6).

In addition to connecting information, hypertext allows the nonlinear organization of information—or organization by association. This is a significant departure from the traditional rhetoric that demands "linear" unity and coherence in text. For example, an essay starts with concept A, then proceeds to B, C, and so on. Each concept is logically or thematically related to its

The ability to communicate with other people and computers worldwide is the Internet's power.

For example, (1) Tom could send e-mail from either his home or university computer to (2) Mary at the Library of Congress LAN, and then (3) obtain a Windows utility program from the Microsoft LAN in Washington.

Note that Tom's home computer can access the Internet via the university or America Online.

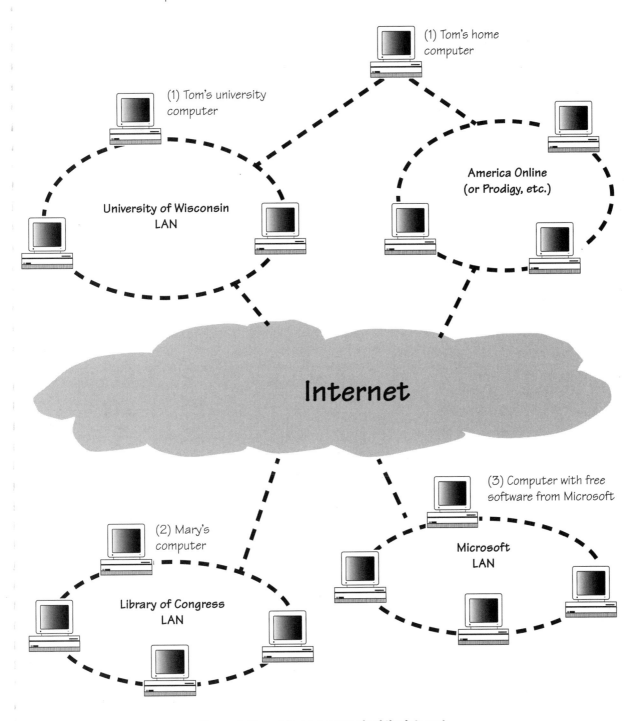

Figure 4: The wide area network of the Internet.

In the beginning there was UNIX, and it was very difficult. Commands had to be typed precisely. There was no room for error.

Next, menu-driven systems made access much easier.

Today's World Wide Web browser software such as Internet Explorer and Netscape invite you to "surf the Net" by using your computer mouse to point and click on hypertext links (the underlined phrases) which allow you to navigate the Web.

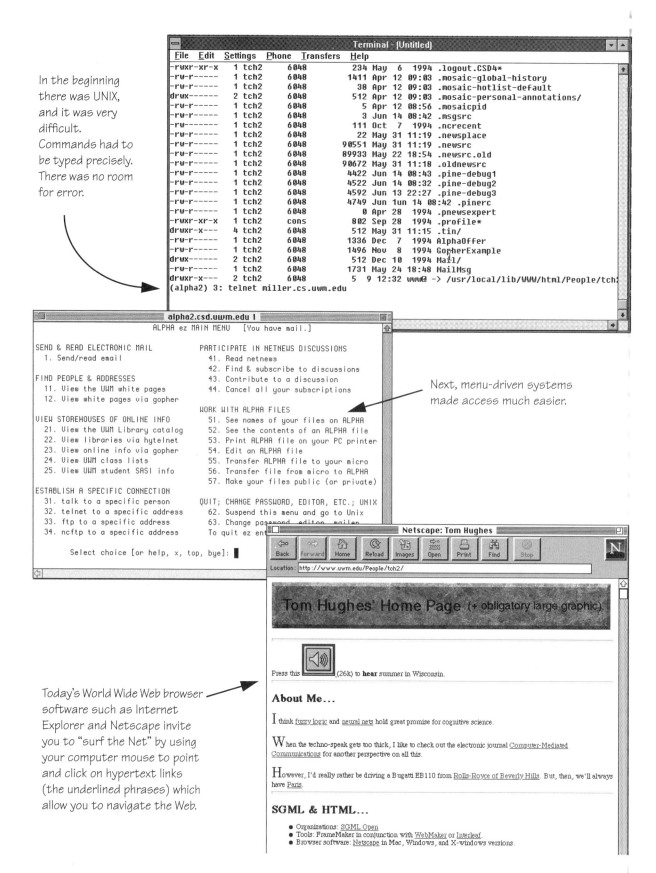

Figure 5: The evolution of Internet access.

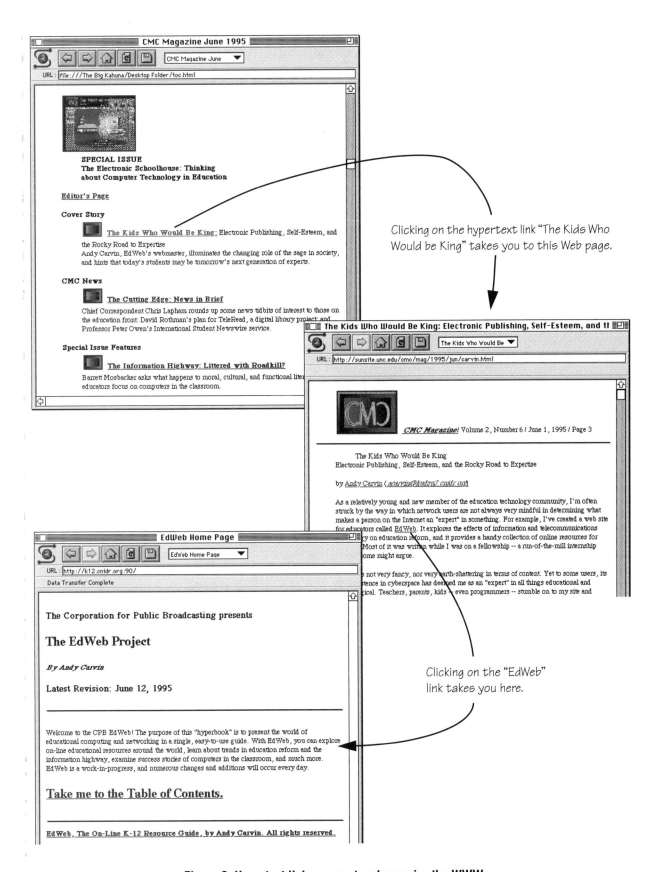

Figure 6: Hypertext links connect and organize the WWW.

predecessor. On the other hand, the nature of hypertext permits and encourages tangents—you may start at A, but before arriving at C (if you ever do), you may stop at Q, L, Y, and W along the way. In addition, hypertext raises questions about where a text begins and ends and the roles of writer and reader.[3] Though challenging the conventions of text, hypertext is not new.

In a 1945 magazine article titled "As We May Think" (http://www.isg.sfu.ca/~duchier/misc/vbush), Dr. Vannevar Bush, the Director of the Office of Scientific Research and Development, described a machine he called the "memex." Bush envisioned the memex as a tool for scientists that would enable them to make sense out of the "growing mountain of research," and he described an example of its possible use:

> The owner of the memex, let us say, is interested in the origin and properties of the bow and arrow. Specifically he is studying why the short Turkish bow was apparently superior to the English long bow in the skirmishes of the Crusades. He has dozens of possible pertinent books and articles in his memex. First he runs through the encyclopedia, finds an interesting but sketchy article, leaves it projected. Next, in a history, he finds another pertinent item, and ties the two together. Thus he goes, building a trail of many items. Occasionally he inserts a comment of his own, either linking it into the main trail or joining it by a side trail to a particular item. When it becomes evident that the elastic properties of the available materials had a great deal to do with the bow, he branches off on a side trail which takes him through textbooks on elasticity and tables of physical constants. He inserts a page of longhand analysis of his own. Thus he builds a trail of his interest through the maze of materials available to him.[4]

This "trail," or connections between ideas, is created by Bush's memex investigator during the course of the research. Though current WWW browsers can automatically keep track of sites visited by a user (Figure 7), the ability to construct meaningful relationships between these locations is beyond the capability of most commercial software today and is still a very human activity. In the near future, search agents and data visualization techniques promise to boost the intelligence of software. Powerful search software (referred to as "search engines") like Lycos (http://www.lycos.com) already exists on the WWW. However, an agent is a much more sophisticated data collector that, in effect, serves as your alter ego. An agent will have the ability to draw inferences and make decisions on its own, but most important, a search agent will be able to learn. In addition, data visualization software will provide three-dimensional spatial representations, or "themescapes," of all the information visited by an Internet browser.[5] For example, **VRML** (Virtual Reality Modeling Language) browsers already are available that allow users to explore information by navigating through virtual worlds. (See "Emerging technologies" for more information.)

Though Bush's memex may have been the precursor of the WWW, it was not the only hypertext implementation prior to

This pull-down list contains all the names (or "Addresses") of the sites the browser visited.

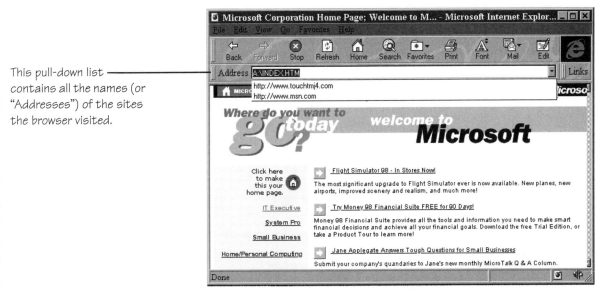

Figure 7: A sample Internet Explorer history list.

Internet Explorer and Netscape. The world's first operational hypertext system was built in 1967 at Brown University.[6]

However, the hypertext application most familiar to teachers is HyperCard (Figure 8). Released in 1987 by Apple, HyperCard's relative ease of use made hypertext authoring accessible to educators. Presentations are created by linking "stacks" of text and graphics.

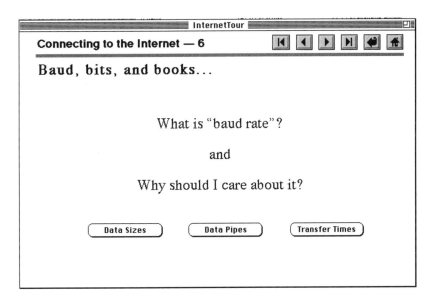

Figure 8: HyperCard example.

 Then in 1989 Tim Berners-Lee created the World Wide Web at CERN, the European Particle Physics Laboratory, in Switzerland, and in January 1993 NCSA, the National Center for Supercomputing Applications, in Illinois released the first edition of the WWW browser Mosaic. Other browsers, like Netscape, were created shortly thereafter.

The amount of traffic on the World Wide Web in January 1993 was 122,440,450 bytes. This equates to sending the complete works of Shakespeare 25 times! (The electronic version of the complete works is about 5 megabytes.) One year later network traffic jumped to 269,129,084,100 bytes (a 219,704% increase!), and in January 1995 it climbed to 3,382,697,720,400 bytes (a 1,157% increase) over the previous year.[7]

WHAT IS ON THE INTERNET?

Types of Internet services

"Everything" is the simplest answer to what is on the Internet, but these are the most common Internet services:

- World Wide Web (WWW)—certainly the most popular Internet service, the WWW gives point-and-click access to the Internet using hypertext to link information together (Figure 9). Also, WWW browser software has evolved to include most of the services just mentioned. For example, the WWW browser Netscape not only allows you to navigate the WWW, but also allows you to create e-mail, subscribe to online discussion groups, and transfer or download text and graphic files to your computer. Unless you love complexity, this multifunctional, or suite, software is very advantageous because it means that you can use one piece of software to do the work of several software applications. In fact the Internet is becoming synonymous with the World Wide Web.

- e-mail—electronic mail allows you to send and receive messages from any one of the millions of people who use the Internet.

- newsgroups—over 10,000 special interest discussion groups that you can join (or "subscribe" to) on everything from education (*misc.education*, *k12.chat.teacher* are the names of two newsgroups) to the extraterrestrial invasion of earth (*alt.alien.visitors*).

- ftp (i.e., file transfer protocol) and Gopher—these two services provide the ability to download information from the Internet to your computer like the complete works of William Shakespeare from the E-*text Archives*, a movie of the planet Mars taken from the H*ubble Space Telescope*, or software that you can use on your Macintosh from Apple (http://www.apple.com) or your Windows-based computer from Microsoft (http://

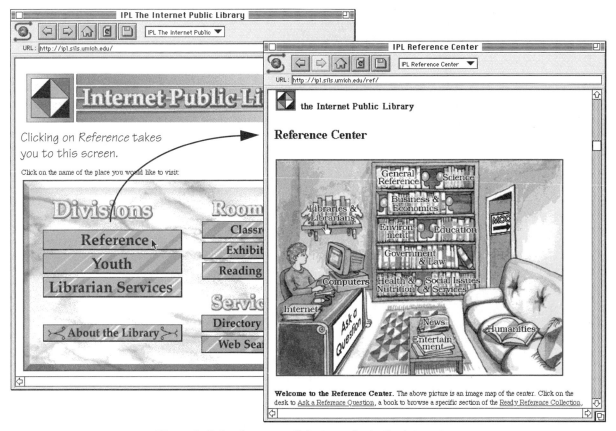

Figure 9: Using hypertext links to navigate the Internet.

www.microsoft.com). However, ftp and gopher are being eclipsed by WWW browsers which automate and effectively replace these two older technologies.

In addition, there are the emerging technologies such as listening to real-time audio—or viewing real-time video—using RealAudio from Progressive Networks (http://www.realaudio.com) and live video conferencing using CU-SeeMe technology developed at New York's Cornell University and commercialized by White Pine Software (http://www.cu-seeme.com).

As you can see, the Internet has a lot to offer educators. Instead of thinking of it as some sort of information superhighway, imagine the Internet as an information warehouse that stores a vast amount of text, graphic, sound, and video data.

Examples of Internet sites of interest to educators

Specifically, here are a few examples of what's available on the Internet of special interest to educators:

- *Web66* (http://web66.coled.umn.edu) describes itself as "a catalyst that will integrate the Internet into K-12 school curricula" and includes a comprehensive list of K-12 schools that are actually on the Internet.

Photo credits: Reta Beebe (New Mexico State University), D. Gilmore, L. Bergeron (STScI), and NASA.

- *Hubble Space Telescope* (http://www.stsci.edu) contains pictures and MPEG[8] movies of planets, stars, galaxies, and other astronomical phenomena.

- *FedWorld* (http://www.fedworld.gov) is an Internet site that is a subject index to the U.S. government and permits you to access information from many agencies and departments.

- *E-text Archives* (www.etext.org[9]) hold electronic versions of many famous texts such as the complete works of William Shakespeare.

- *The Library of Congress* (http://lcweb.loc.gov) National Digital Library contains life history manuscripts from the WPA Federal Writers' Folklore Project, Civil War photographs by Mathew Brady, and early motion pictures that include a movie of San Francisco after the 1906 earthquake.

- *White House* (http://www.whitehouse.gov) has text and pictures about the first family as well as an audio recording of first cat Socks.

- CIA *World Factbook* (http://www.odci.gov/cia/publications/pub.html) is an encyclopedic data source on every country in the world. Where else could you find the electrical capacity of the Cayman Islands? (It's 74,000 kW.)

 **National Oceanic and Atmospheric Administration**

- *Weather Information Superhighway* (http://thunder.met.fsu.edu/~nws/wxhwy.html) is a service of the National Weather Service containing weather forecasts as well as current visible and infrared satellite images. However, a commercial weather site such as *The Weather Channel* (http:///www.weather.com) may offer information that is more accessible to younger students.

Also, with a little effort you can even add your own information to the Internet (see Chapter 4).

MISUSE OF THE INTERNET

Netiquette

Netiquette is Internet etiquette, informal rules that have evolved into guidelines of good conduct. Consideration for others is netiquette's premise. These "rules of the road" are important for all Internet users to learn, especially younger ones, because the bad or ignorant behavior of one student or teacher could jeopardize the Internet privileges of others. Though using netiquette may be desirable, it is not required. However, ignorance of netiquette could make you look foolish or, worse, draw the wrath of other Internet users.

SHOUTING, **flaming**, and **spamming** are three common examples of bad netiquette that should be avoided.

SHOUTING

SHOUTING is the overuse of capital letters. There's nothing wrong with using capitalization to call attention to an occasional word or phase. However, when used too often or indiscriminately, it makes reading e-mail difficult. SHOUTING may be a minor irritation, but it still hampers effective communication.

Flaming

Flaming is an e-mail attack on someone. Reading an e-mail flame is like listening to an angry person argue—it's not pleasant because the words are intended to annoy or hurt someone. Consider the following message taken verbatim from an education newsgroup:

```
One experience I had at Fla. State Univ. was knowing some
"EDUCATION MAJORS." They knew nothing except how to teach,
which meant their knowledge was totally lacking in
substance. Nice people, no guts, no brains.

It wasn't long after that experience that the Fla.
legislature requried that these Educ. Majors learn something
OTHER than how to write a lesson plan (big challenge being
organized).
```

Though the line between vigorous debating and flaming may be fuzzy, these are some common characteristics of flaming:

- personal attacks or baiting,
- overly long e-mail messages, and
- repeated e-mail messages on the same topic.

Bear in mind that these are general guidelines. There are newsgroups on the Internet where flaming is invited and even expected.

Spamming

Putting, or "posting," the same e-mail message on many newsgroups is called spamming and is not considered proper netiquette. For example, in 1994 Arizona lawyers Laurence Canter and Martha Siegel sent a message to nearly every newsgroup offering their services for the U.S. Green Card Lottery. Their action outraged many Internet users who bombarded the Internet service provider of the two lawyers with e-mail. At first, the service provider terminated their account, but Canter and Siegel threatened to sue. The Internet provider restored service after the two lawyers agreed to refrain from mass postings.[10]

Most cases of bad netiquette behavior are not this extreme. For example, when new Internet users, who are called **newbies**, visit newsgroups, they often ask questions before taking the time to look at other messages for their answer or investigating the newsgroup's **FAQ** (Frequently Asked Questions). An FAQ is an electronic text file containing commonly asked questions and their answers, and many but not all newsgroups provide an FAQ file.

If all else fails, "**lurk**" before you leap. Lurking is Internet jargon that means if you are new to the Internet, it is best to watch how others behave before doing anything yourself.

Because netiquette is a set of guidelines rather than rules written in stone, a frequently cited netiquette code is included in Appendix A as a starting point.

Safety and objectionable materials

The Internet has a dark side. Newspaper and television stories frequently appear about some child who downloaded pornographic pictures or who was enticed by e-mail into a meeting with a pedophile. Even the language used in some newsgroups is very rough and is definitely not for young children.

Currently there are no fail-safe methods of protecting students from all this. However, Internet providers should be able to "lock out" students from specified sites. Also, there are commercial programs available like SurfWatch (http://www.surfwatch.com/) and Microsystems Software CyberPatrol/CyberSentry (http://www.microsys.com) (Figure 10) that offer more sophisticated lockout capabilities. For example, SurfWatch filters what can be viewed by using a database of Internet sites considered inappropriate for students.

The following guidelines may protect students from the most serious abuses:

- Students should understand basic netiquette.

- While using the Internet, but especially for newsgroup and e-mail correspondence, students should be monitored. Base monitoring on the age—the younger the student, the more monitoring. (The Macintosh and Windows software Timbuktu Pro[11] permits the greatest control over what students can see. This software makes it possible for all the computers on a network to watch what is happening on the screen of another computer. For example, a teacher could demonstrate how to use e-mail software by creating an e-mail message on his or her computer. Using Timbuktu Pro, the teacher's e-mail message would appear on each student's computer screen. Timbuktu Pro is an excellent tool for direct instruction and demonstrations.)

- Students should be directed to never give out personal information such as their phone number, address, and so on over the Internet.

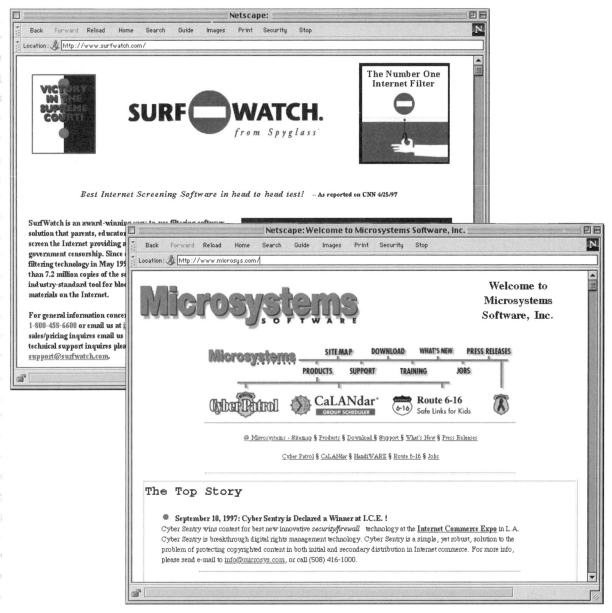

Figure 10: SurfWatch and CyberSentry/CyberPatrol are software applications available for both Macintosh and Windows that offer methods of restricting student access to objectionable Internet sites.

Even with the best type of site lockout, you should develop an **Acceptable Use Policy (AUP)**. An AUP is a set of rights and responsibilities that is specifically written for Internet users in your school or institution. Whereas netiquette is a set of guidelines for using the Internet, an AUP is a set of rules. Violating an AUP could result in a person losing Internet access. This is why some schools have made their AUP into a contract that the user must sign. Parents, teachers, students, administrators, and your Internet provider should be included in drafting an AUP.

HOW DO YOU GET ON THE INTERNET?

To connect your home or school computers to the Internet you need to know about **Internet service providers** and the speed, or baud rate, of your connection.

Internet service providers

Whether you want to hook up a single home computer or an entire school full of computers, you have to go through an Internet service provider to get on the Internet. Universities are often service providers and may offer free Internet access to students, staff, and alumni. For example, in Figure 4 Tom uses two computers that are on the Internet, one at his home, the other at school. One of the Internet service providers for his home computer is a university that doesn't charge him anything since he's a student. However, Tom also uses a commercial Internet service provider at home, America Online.

Commercial Internet service providers are another way to connect to the Internet. Generally, they charge a monthly fee based on how *fast* a connection you want. The faster the Internet connection, the more you pay. There are regional and national providers. For example, AT&T (http://www.att.com), America Online (http://www.aol.com), GEnie (http://www.genie.com), and Prodigy (http://www.prodigy.com) are national Internet service providers because they are available in most parts of the United States. On the other hand, regional Internet service providers serve a much smaller area, like one or two states or even just a city.

Be certain to comparison shop for an Internet service provider because prices can vary drastically. *MacWorld* magazine compared the price charged by all the major national Internet service providers for "light," "moderate," and "heavy" use and found wide variations.[12]

Appendix C contains a list of national Internet service providers, but for an up-to-date list of regional Internet service providers, use the WWW to see the Providers of Commercial Internet Access (POCIA) (http://www.celestin.com/pocia/).

Internet connection speed

You can use a personal computer with a modem attached to an ordinary phone line to access the Internet, as Tom did from his home computer in Figure 4. This is referred to as a "dial-up" connection and it is usually slow. On the other hand, if you want to connect computers on a LAN at your school to the Internet, a permanent or "dedicated" connection to the Internet is the most cost-effective solution. The dedicated connection is much faster than the dial-up.

This connection speed is called the **baud rate**. Internet baud rates typically range from 28,800 baud (or 28.8 Kbps), a typical modem, to 44.736 megabaud (or 44.736 Mbps), a high-speed LAN connection to the Internet. An interesting note: in the first edition of this book, a 28.8 Kbps was a fast dial-up connection. Now it's just considered typical as the demand for faster and faster communication increases. Also, 56 Kbps used to be considered a *network* speed, but today dial-up modems can achieve this speed.

Why should you care about baud rate? It boils down to time and money—*your* time and *your* money. But first, it might be easier to understand Internet connection speed by imagining baud rates as varying sizes of data "pipes" (Figure 11). The bigger the pipe, the more data that can be transported. And just like plumbing, one size does not fit all.

Type of data	Size[A]	Time required to transfer data from the Internet to your computer			
		Dial-up speeds (in kilobaud[B])		Network speeds (in kilobaud)	
		28.8[C]	56	1,544[D]	44,736[E]
Graphic of Lincoln	53 KB	15 sec	7.5 sec	0.3 sec	0.009 sec
Sound recording of Neil Armstrong saying, "That's one small step for man, one giant leap for mankind."	68 KB	19 sec	10 sec	0.4 sec	0.012 sec
24-second MPEG movie of the planet Mars spinning	755 KB	3.5 min	2 min	4 sec	0.14 sec
24-second QuickTime movie of the planet Mars spinning	8.4 MB	40 min	20 min	44 sec	1.5 sec

NOTES:
A. "KB" means kilobyte and "MB" means megabyte. Both measure the size of data.
B. "Baud" means bits per second (bps) and measures how fast data is moving.
C. 28.8 and 56 kilobaud are data transfer speeds attainable in off-the-shelf computer modems. Though a lower speed modem could be used to access the Internet, it's not recommended because most of your time on the Internet will be spent *waiting* for data to arrive.
D. This is usually referred to as a "T1" connection and is an increasingly common connection speed delivered to businesses and schools.
E. This is usually referred to as a "T3" connection.

Table 1: Why you should care about baud rate.

Second, keep in mind that the Internet is a multimedia network and includes not just textual information, but also graphics, sounds, and videos that contain more data—that is, they're "bigger"—than ordinary text. For example, a text file made up of the sentence "That's one small step for man, one giant leap for mankind" takes up only a few bytes, but a sound recording of these words will take up thousands of bytes. Using the baud pipe analogy, though a few bytes flow through a small baud pipe in no time at all, getting thousands of bytes through takes much longer.

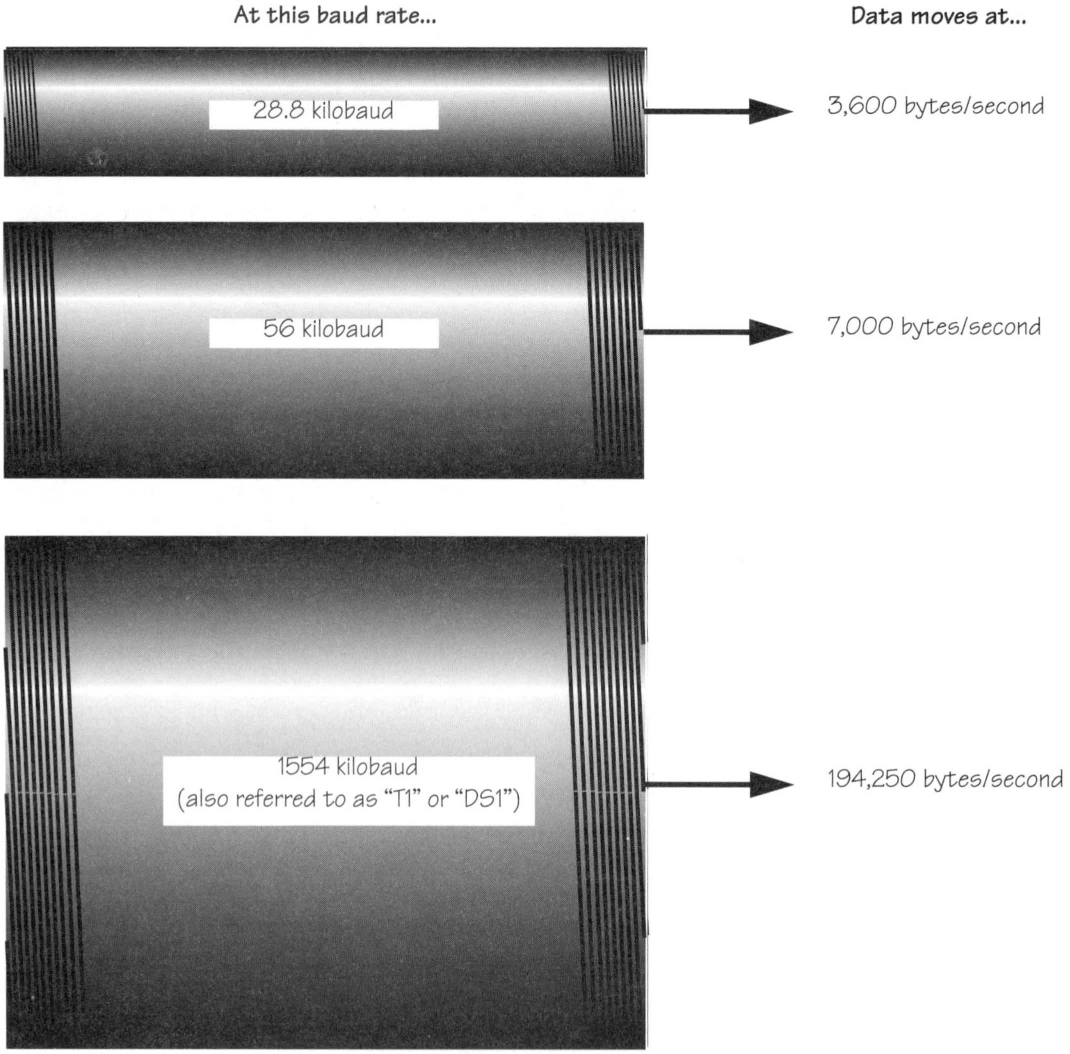

At this baud rate...   Data moves at...

28.8 kilobaud

3,600 bytes/second

56 kilobaud

7,000 bytes/second

1554 kilobaud
(also referred to as "T1" or "DS1")

194,250 bytes/second

Figure 11: Baud rate "pipes."

To understand the implications of baud rate and multimedia data, look at the samples in Table 1 of various kinds of data on the Internet and how long it takes to move them to your computer. What should be obvious from the table is that even with the fastest dial-up connection of 56 Kbps, it might be prudent to schedule your dining times during movie downloads as it takes from 20 minutes up to 40 minutes for the average QuickTime[13] movie (shaded areas in Table 1).

We can safely say from experience that using a 28.8 Kbps modem on the Internet, though certainly not an ideal setup, does provide bearable dial-up access. However, because it does take longer to download information, you may find this too slow in the classroom setting. Having students waiting for a downloaded file can consume precious classroom time. Therefore, you may consider a faster *network* connection.

There is hope for speedy and economical school and home

Internet connections. By the time you read this, public and private initiatives are well under way to deliver fast network connection speeds to schools.

Home Internet connections

Method 1: Modem dial-up setup (1 computer ← 1 ordinary phone line)

This configuration (Figure 12) provides you with basic Internet service. With it you can send e-mail, subscribe to newsgroups, use WWW browsers, and view or download text, images, sounds, and movies. Table 2 outlines what you'll need for a basic home connection to the Internet.

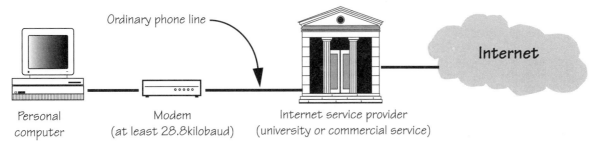

Figure 12: Basic home connection.

Hardware:	Computers:	Windows: Pentium
		Macintosh: PowerPC
	Modem:	28.8 Kbps (minimum)
Software:	Windows:	Netscape, Internet Explorer (for WWW)
		Pine, Eudora, or WWW browser (for e-mail)
		Windows 95 software
	Macintosh:	Netscape, Internet Explorer (for WWW)
		Pine, Eudora, or WWW browser (for e-mail)
		Macintosh System 8 software
Internet Service Provider:	either a university or a commercial provider who offers dial-up PPP service	
Cost:	Monthly:	Free to $15 (Universities are a source of free Internet service.)
	One time:	$150 for 56 Kbps modem
	NOTE: Educational versions of Netscape, Internet Explorer, and Eudora software are free.	

Table 2: Basic home connection needs.

Method 2: ISDN dial-up setup (1 computer ← 1 ISDN phone line)

The **ISDN** setup (see Figure 13 and Table 3) provides all the services found in Method 1, but is much faster—up to 128 Kbps. What makes this affordable is the fact that the ISDN connection is not permanent as in a network, but rather a dial-up.[14]

Be aware that setting up ISDN involves a healthy dose of rocket science caused in part by the fact that it is not standardized across the country. Ask your local telephone company and Internet service provider a lot of questions before pursuing an ISDN connection. For example, make sure

- the terminal adapter (i.e., the ISDN "modem") you will purchase is compatible with your service provider, and

- you understand how much your telephone company and service provider will charge you for their services.

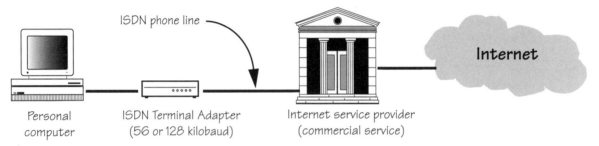

Figure 13: ISDN setup.

Hardware:	Computers:	Windows: Pentium Macintosh: PowerPC
	Modem:	Motorola BitSURFR PRO terminal adapter or similar Also, there are ISDN "routers" available that let you share the single ISDN connection with multiple computers.
Software:	Windows:	Netscape, Internet Explorer (for WWW) Pine, Eudora, or WWW browser (for e-mail) Windows 95 software
	Macintosh:	Netscape, Internet Explorer (for WWW) Pine, Eudora, or WWW browser (for e-mail) Macintosh System 8 software
Internet Service Provider:	commercial provider who offers ISDN service	
Cost:	Monthly:	$50+ split between your local telephone company and your Internet service provider
	One time:	$300+ for ISDN terminal adapter such as a Motorola BitSURFR PRO $120+ to have your local telephone company install an ISDN connection
		NOTE: Educational versions of Netscape, Internet Explorer, and Eudora software are free.

Table 3: ISDN setup needs.

School Internet connections

Method 1: "We just want to get our feet wet." (1 computer ← 1 phone line)

Many educators are hesitant to spend thousands of dollars installing a full networked Internet connection in their schools. If this is your situation, then explore the modem dial-up or ISDN setups mentioned previously. Though these two methods restrict the number of computers that can be connected to the Internet at any one time, they do allow cost-effective experimentation. Though limited, this "pilot" approach should still raise questions you will need to address before undertaking a more complete Internet installation. For example:

- How will teacher Internet training be handled?

- Who will be responsible for network administration? That is, who do you call when a computer or the network crashes? Is there a designated teacher, or administrator, or student? (This provides great justification for student involvement as administering a computer network provides very authentic instruction.)

- Will teachers, students, or the local community be allowed to access the school's Internet connection from their homes?

- What will be in your Acceptable Use Policy (AUP)? Will you have students sign contracts stating what they can and cannot do on the Internet? How will you police and enforce such contracts?

- What sort of Internet security do you want? Do you want the ability to block out certain Internet sites from students?

Method 2: "We want it all!" (*Many* computers ← 1 digital phone line)

Connecting the computers in one or more schools to the Internet requires a sizeable investment of both time and money. You will have to balance your wishes with what you can afford. For example, if your school's computers are not connected to a LAN, they should be. Installation of a LAN requires "pulling" cables through walls, ceilings, and basements, and is an extremely labor-intensive task. By the way, if you're thinking of doing it yourself—don't. Wiring a network is a job for experts, not weekend warriors.

A detailed description of how to connect a school to the Internet is beyond the scope of this book. However, as a starting point, read *Connecting to the Internet* by Susan Estrada, published by O'Reilly & Associates, Inc. (They put out a number of fine books about the Internet.) Also, contact local schools that have already established an Internet connection. If there are no schools close by, find someone with an Internet connection (e.g., a local university) and use a WWW browser like Internet Explorer or Netscape to go to *Web66* (http://web66.coled.umn.edu). This Internet site has a list of schools across the country that have Internet service. Contact these schools for their insights.

Remember to plan for the future. You're really not saving money by building a LAN for 25 computers when you soon expect to expand to 100.

Because of the complexity and variety of possible network configurations, Figure 14 represents only one of many ways in which a single school may be connected to the Internet. For example, network "firewalls" information is completely absent. (A *firewall* is software and hardware used to restrict access to and from the Internet and is typically used to prevent computer hackers from breaking into your network.) Table 4 lists hardware and software requirements as well as approximate costs for such a connection.

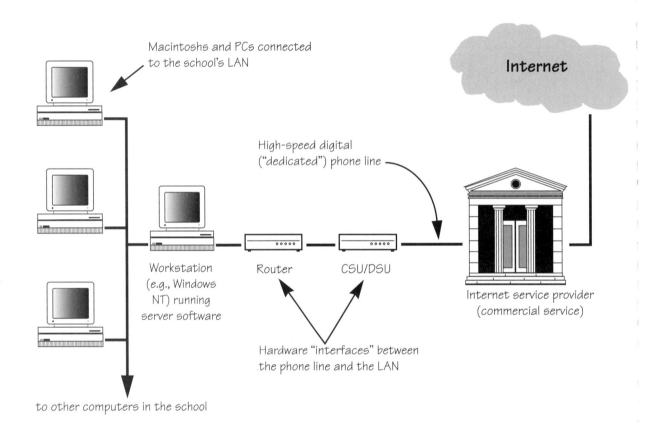

Figure 14: Connecting a school LAN to the Internet.

Hardware:	Computers:	Windows: Pentium Macintosh: PowerPC
	Workstation:	PowerPC, Pentium PC, Windows NT, Sun SPARC for running the Internet communications software
	Router:	connects the school LAN to the Internet
	CSU/DSU:	converts phone line data into something the Router understands
Software:	Windows:	Netscape, Internet Explorer (for WWW) Pine, Eudora, or WWW browser (for e-mail) Windows 95 software
	Macintosh:	Netscape, Internet Explorer (for WWW) Pine, Eudora, or WWW browser (for e-mail) Macintosh System 8 software
	Workstation:	Internet communications software such as Netscape Suite Spot (for UNIX and Windows NT) or Webstar (for Macintosh)
Internet Service Provider:		commercial provider who offers high-speed Internet connection (such as T1)
Cost:	Monthly:	$100+ to local telephone company for a high-speed phone line $500+ to Internet service provider for high-speed Internet connection
	One-time:	$1000+ for Router $400+ for CSD/DSU $3000 fee split between your local telephone company and your Internet service provider to install the high-speed phone line to a school $2000 for Internet communications software (e.g., Netscape Suite Spot)
		NOTE: Educational versions of Netscape, Internet Explorer, and Eudora software are free.

Table 4: School LAN connection needs.

INTERNET SOFTWARE

Software for using the Internet continues to evolve at a rapid pace and there are bound to be changes from what appears on the following pages. So if you can't find the software we mention either here or later on in our book, search for the software on one of the many Internet shareware libraries, like C/NET (http://www.shareware.com and www.download.com).

This section provides examples of e-mail, WWW browser, audio conferencing, video conferencing, virtual reality, and Java software, most of which is available in both Windows and Macintosh versions.

At the time this book was written, a trend toward integrated, or suite, software (e.g., Netscape) was well under way. Suite software is a single piece of software that can create and send e-mail, read newsgroups, browse the World Wide Web, and perform other functions.

Connection software

Connection software used to be the "rocket science" of getting onto the Internet and was more like *plug and pray* than plug and play. However, since the first edition of this book, there have been significant improvements in making this process easier.

To get on the Internet, a TCP/IP connection must be established between your computer and your Internet Service Provider. If a dial-up connection will be used, then you'll need PPP (Point-to-Point Protocol) software. On the other hand, if a network connection like Ethernet will be used, then you'll need Ethernet software and hardware. Both Windows 95 and Macintosh System 8 have TCP/IP and PPP in their software. Also, most Macintoshes have Ethernet built in. (Windows PCs will need a special Ethernet card installed.)

For either a LAN or a home connection to the Internet, the following software will be needed:

Macintosh connection software

Open Transport software—part of System 8—must be installed on a Macintosh.

TCP/IP

TCP is a Macintosh control panel (Figure 15) which you must configure in order for it to work properly. To do this, contact your Internet service provider and ask for setup instructions for MacTCP.

NOTE: PPP has replaced a SLIP (Serial Line Interface Protocol) connection to the Internet.

A TCP/IP connection uses either the PPP (for dial-up access) or the Ethernet (for network access) protocol.

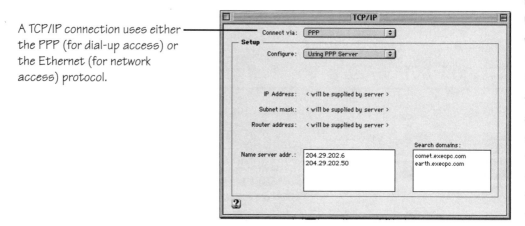

Figure 15: TCP/IP control panel.

PPP

PPP (Figure 16) is a control panel used to establish a PPP or dial-up Internet connection.

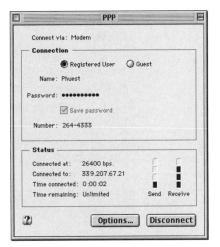

Figure 16: PPP control panel.

Windows connection software

Installing and using TCP/IP and PPP software on a Windows PC is similar to a Macintosh because in a Windows environment, control panels are also used to set up connections (see Figure 17).

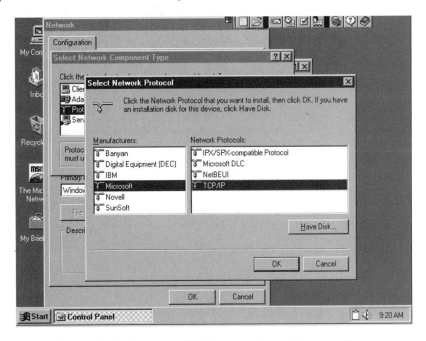

Figure 17: Setting up a TCP/IP connection in Windows 95.

Telnet software

Telnet software is referred to as "terminal emulation" software and is used to display text-only information. Only primitive graphics can be displayed on a telnet application. The terms "VT100," "VT102," "VT220," and so on are often used in conjunction with telnet software and represent different standards for displaying text on the screen.

Though graphical Internet applications like Netscape and Internet Explorer are the most popular method of displaying information on the Internet, telnet software is still necessary. For example, most universities (especially libraries) must be accessed using telnet.

The easiest method of obtaining either Windows or Macintosh Telnet software is via the Internet using the Tucows WWW site (http://www.tucows.com) (Figure 18).

Figure 18: The Tucows WWW site is an excellent source of Telnet (and other Internet) software.

E-mail software

Electronic mail, or **e-mail**, which will be covered extensively in Chapter 2, is the most fundamental Internet application. E-mail is the process of composing text on one computer and then sending that text to one or more persons via a computer network. E-mail can be used to communicate with anyone on the Internet, which means anyone in the world. It is an excellent method of having students communicate with others.

In ordinary conversation and in telephone calls (without using an answering machine), communication takes place only if there is a person in front of you or at the other end of the phone line when you talk or place the phone call. This type of communication is synchronous—sender and receiver must be present at the same time. E-mail is probably the most powerful Internet tool because it allows asynchronous communication. E-mail is like leaving a message with a telephone answering machine. Your conversation is stored and will be "read" (and possibly replied to) when the owner of the machine gets around to it.

Two e-mail software applications are considered in this chapter:

- Pine (Table 5) is a program that runs on your Internet service provider's computer but not your home computer. However, to use Pine you do need software on your computer, like a terminal emulation program or NCSA Telnet (for Macintosh and DOS).

- Eudora (Table 6, Figure 20) is a feature-packed e-mail software program that operates on your Macintosh or Windows personal computer. A free version is available for educational use.

Pine

Purpose:	e-mail program
Platform:	usually runs on your Internet service provider's computer
Where to get:	University of Washington at Seattle WWW site:　http://www.cac.washington.edu/pine/ ftp site:　　ftp://ftp.cac.washington.edu/pine/
Price:	Free
Notes:	In order to use Pine, you'll need to run a telnet program (see previous section on telnet software) on your computer.

Table 5: Pine information.

Pine is an e-mail program that typically runs on UNIX computers. It is not a very user-friendly program when compared with Windows or Macintosh, but it is included because university Internet service providers are likely to use Pine. The University of Washington, the creators of Pine, report that 4,000 sites in 40 countries have downloaded the latest version.

Basic operation of Pine is shown in Figure 19. Note that you must first start your terminal emulation program or NCSA Telnet on your computer and then dial-up your Internet service provider. The Internet address of the service provider—alpha2.csd.uwm.edu— appears in the screens in Figure 19.

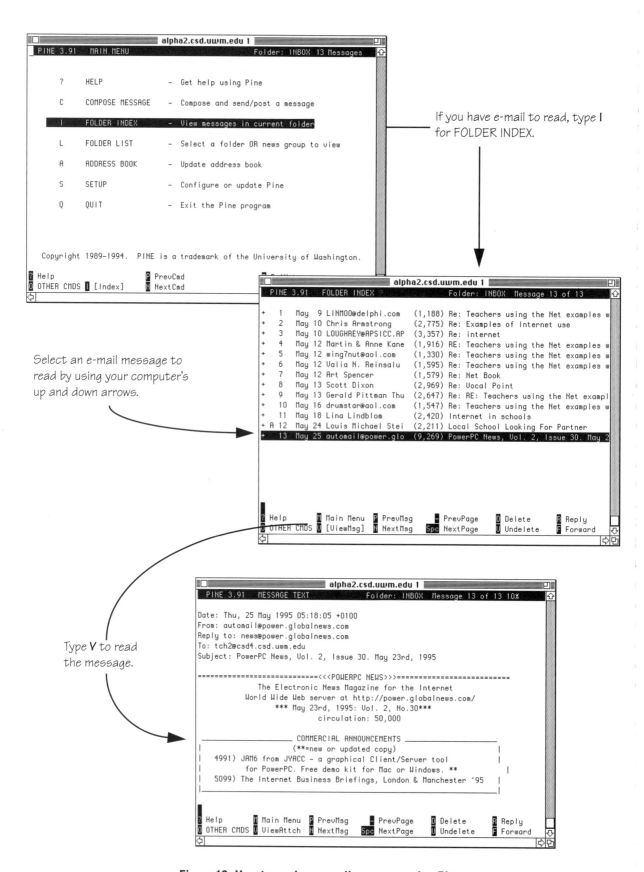

Figure 19: How to read an e-mail message using Pine.

Eudora Light

Purpose:	e-mail program
Platform:	Windows, Macintosh
Where to get:	QUALCOMM Enterprise Software Technologies (QUEST) 6455 Lusk Blvd. San Diego, CA 92121 (800) 2-EUDORA WWW site: http://www.eudora.com ftp site: ftp.eudora.com
Price:	Free (There is also a retail version available called Eudora Pro for about $60 that has more features than the free version.)

Table 6: Eudora information.

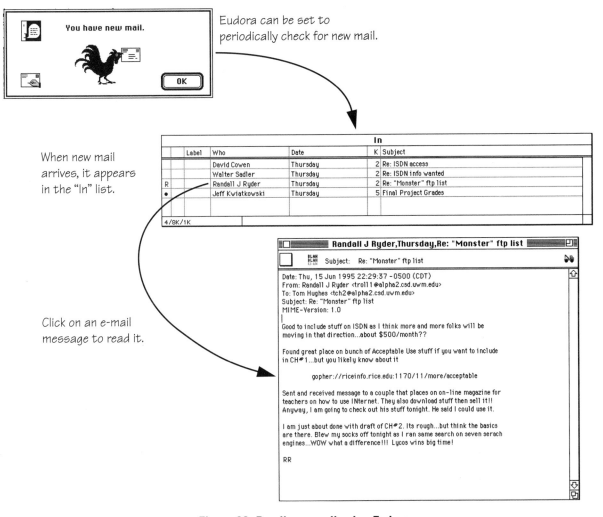

Eudora can be set to periodically check for new mail.

When new mail arrives, it appears in the "In" list.

Click on an e-mail message to read it.

Figure 20: Reading e-mail using Eudora.

World Wide Web (WWW) browser software

WWW browser software, browsers for short, are necessary to use the Internet's World Wide Web. Browsers can be used over network or dial-up Internet connections. Descriptions of two of the most popular browsers—Netscape and Internet Explorer—are given in Figures 21-23 and Tables 7-8.

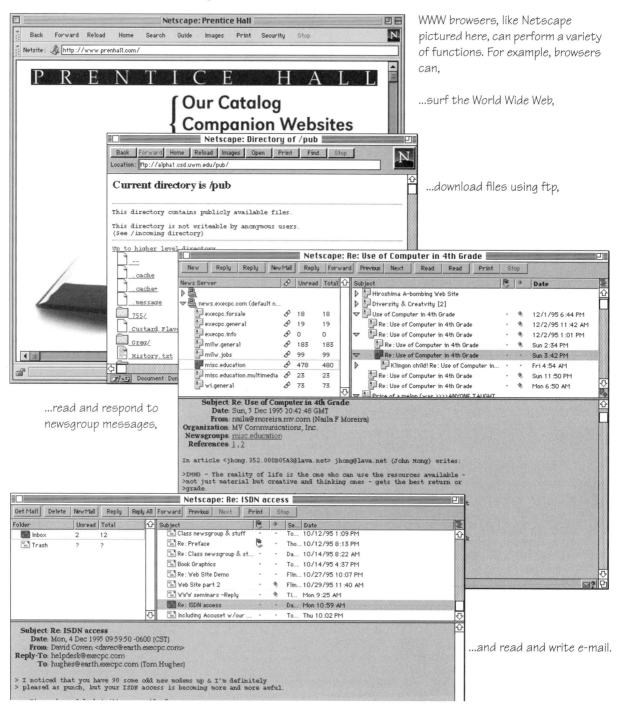

WWW browsers, like Netscape pictured here, can perform a variety of functions. For example, browsers can,

...surf the World Wide Web,

...download files using ftp,

...read and respond to newsgroup messages,

...and read and write e-mail.

Figure 21: WWW browsers like Netscape are multifunctional.

Netscape Navigator

Purpose:	World Wide Web browser
Platform:	Windows, Macintosh, Sun, SGI, DEC, HP

Where to get:	Netscape Communications Corporation
	(415) 528-2555
	(415) 528-4140 (fax)
	WWW site: http://www.netscape.com
	ftp site: ftp://ftp.netscape.com
	                ftp://ftp2.netscape.com
	                ftp://ftp3.netscape.com/pub
	                ftp://wuarchive.wustl.edu/packages/www/

Price:	Free (There is also a retail version of Netscape available.)

Table 7: Netscape Navigator information.

Netscape holds the title of the most popular WWW browser.

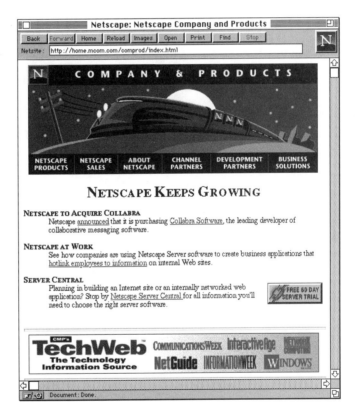

Figure 22: Netscape WWW browser.

Microsoft's Internet Explorer

Between the first and second edition of this book, Microsoft's WWW browser—Internet Explorer—has taken the Internet by storm. Though Netscape Navigator is still the most widely used WWW browser, Internet Explorer is definitely number two. Regardless of which one you use, either is a powerhouse of features.

NOTE: NCSA's Mosaic, the first WWW browser, is just not used enough to warrant mentioning.

Purpose:	World Wide Web browser
Platform:	Windows, Macintosh
Where to get:	WWW site: http://www.microsoft.com ftp site: ftp.microsoft.com
Price:	Free

Table 8: Internet Explorer information.

Internet Explorer is Microsoft's WWW browser.

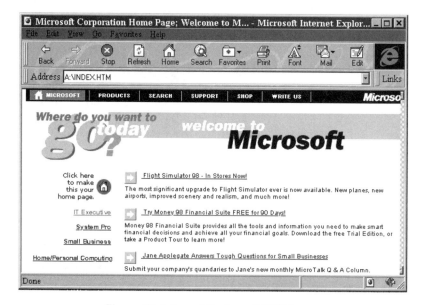

Figure 23: Internet Explorer WWW browser.

Emerging technologies

Three promising areas of new Internet technology are audio conferencing, video conferencing, and virtual reality.

Audio conferencing

IRC (Internet Relay Chat) is the precursor to real-time audio conferencing. IRC lets users on other Internet computers see what is typed on your screen. Though IRC allows Internet users to communicate in real time, IRC is not true audio conferencing because you must type the words you want to say instead of speaking them. However, new applications like NetPhone (Figure 24) are making two-way spoken communication possible over the Internet.

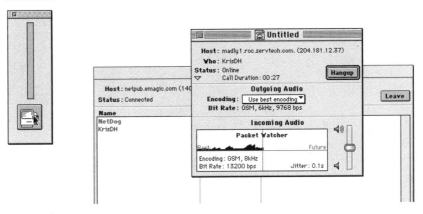

Figure 24: NetPhone audio conferencing software.

Video conferencing

Video conferencing typically requires a very fast (384 Kbps or faster) Internet connection in order to be effective. At speeds below this, the motion on the screen may be jerky and the sound may break up. Nevertheless, at slow speeds relatively stationary objects (or people) can be displayed on a computer screen. For example, many people broadcast images of themselves over the Internet by mounting an inexpensive black-and-white video camera on top of their computer monitor and using a software application called CU-SeeMe (see Figure 25 and Table 9).

CU-SeeMe software allows computers equipped with video cameras to communicate with each other using live video and audio. Though the quality of the video and audio is not very good, you are able to send and receive video images from people all over the world. Each person appears in a small window on your computer.

Purpose:	desktop video conferencing
Platform:	Windows, Macintosh
Where to get:	White Pine Software: phone: (603)-886-9050 e-mail: info@wpine.com WWW: http://www.wpine.com
Price:	Free (A commercial version is also available.)

Table 9: CU-SeeMe information.

Figure 25: CU-SeeMe home page.

Virtual reality

Virtual reality software gives the impression of three-dimensional interaction. Computer game software like Doom and Descent are similar because they give the illusion of operating in three-dimensional space.

A special WWW language called VRML (Virtual Reality Modeling Language) has been developed. It is used by Internet virtual reality software like WebSpace (Table 10 and Figure 26).

Purpose:	3D access to Internet VRML information
Platform:	Windows, Macintosh, Sun, SGI, DEC, HP
Where to get:	Silicon Graphics, Inc. WWW site: http://www.sgi.com/Products/products.html
Price:	Free.

Table 10: WebSpace information.

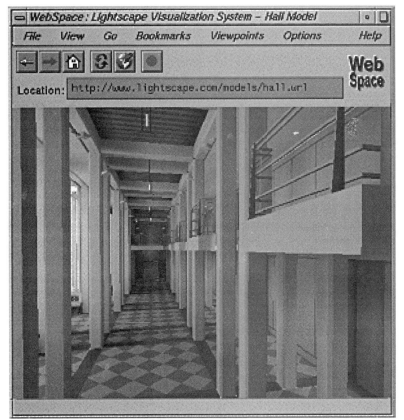

Figure 26: WebSpace.

Java

Java is a very powerful programming language that—according to its developers at Sun Microsystems (http://www.sun.com)—allows WWW browsers to do just about anything. Though this claim may be a bit overstated, a Java-enabled WWW browser like Netscape should be able to do anything from displaying online spreadsheets to performing complex graphical operations.

Java promises to usher in not only a new era of WWW development but also a new era of computing by combining the capabilities of desktop and network computers. Currently, when you use a program on a desktop computer, you purchase a single copy of it and put it on your computer's hard disk drive. However, Java makes it possible for a computer program to reside on a *network* instead of on your personal computer. This is a fundamental difference. For example, in the future you may never *buy* a computer program—you may *rent* it over a network and pay a fee based on what type of program it is and how long you use it.

InTRAnets — BRINGING THE OUTSIDE IN

An Intranet is a network set up inside a school or business to behave just like the Internet with one notable exception—while the Internet is available to anyone, an Intranet is a *private* network (Figure 27). A school Intranet would typically be used by just the students and staff in that particular school. No one from the outside (i.e., the Internet) would be let in. By the same token, no one inside the school would be allowed out.

This means that students could not access the vast information stores on the Net, nor could they communicate with anyone over the Internet. This is no small loss. However, there are several benefits in setting up an Intranet:

- Security—With no connection to the Internet, students could not access objectionable material like pornography. Even with the most stringent monitoring, the shear number of Internet sites makes it impossible for teachers to check all the content of student searchers.

- Cost—Since there is no Internet access, there are no costs for hooking the school up to an Internet Service Provider, and there are no monthly costs for Internet access. While there are costs associated with the cabling necessary to operate an Intranet, there are no costs for security software, routers, and so on.

- Relevance—The Internet does have everything, but much of it is not only irrelevant, but distracting, to students. An Intranet permits the control of content.

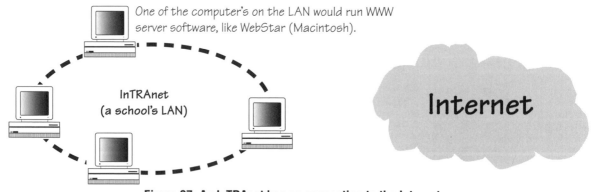

One of the computer's on the LAN would run WWW server software, like WebStar (Macintosh).

InTRAnet
(a school's LAN)

Internet

Figure 27: An InTRAnet has no connection to the Internet.

CONCLUDING REMARKS

This chapter has presented an overview of the components of the Internet, misuses of the Internet, methods of getting connected to the Internet, and a description of the software used to access the Internet. In closing, we would like to emphasize three major points raised in this chapter.

The first point addresses the concept of connectivity. Because the Internet is a network of networks uniting computers and people around the world, it provides a system for communicating that allows anyone with a computer, a modem, a few pieces of software, and a service provider to connect to the worldwide resources of the Net. And with the widespread use and success of user-friendly browser software, individuals can cruise the Internet with ease.

A second point deals with access. The point-and-click environment of hypertext available on the World Wide Web allows easy access to data on the Internet and it permits rapid access to information acquired in a nonlinear manner. Access to the Internet itself has become more readily available with an increase in the number of regional and national service providers. Thus no matter where you live, access to the Internet can be obtained by dialing into local or toll-free national telephone numbers.

A third and final point raised in this chapter deals with appropriate behavior and use of the Internet. Even though the pornographic and obscene material on the Net has been overemphasized by the media, anyone with a basic knowledge of navigating the Net can readily acquire this sort of information. As a result of the increasing use of the Internet by school-age children, methods such as software tools are being developed to lock out students from objectionable sites. Additionally, educators are urged to develop an Acceptable Use Policy that addresses these and other issues and to work closely with their service provider to screen out unwanted services. However, a private Internet—or Intranet—could be set up in a school to alleviate many of these fears.

ACTIVITIES

1. Who uses the WWW?

The Graphics, Visualization, and Usability Center (GVU) at the Georgia Institute of Technology has surveyed WWW users in order to get a picture of who uses the Internet (http://www.gatech.edu/pitkow/survey).

- Download one of these GVU surveys and describe the typical WWW user.
- Download at least two GVU surveys and describe how the typical WWW user has changed over time.

2. Writing an AUP

If you were responsible for drafting an Acceptable Use Policy for a high school,

- what sort of information would you be sure to include?
- what sort of things would you exclude?

3. Dealing with objectionable material

Because you may be in a position where you must decide what is and what is not appropriate material for students, read the following e-mail conversation taken from the k12.chat.teacher newsgroup[15] and respond to the following questions:

- How would you answer Elizabeth?
- Do you prefer John or Ben's solution? Why?
- How would you respond to Jane's message?
- How would your responses differ for grade school, high school, and university students?

Elizabeth:

```
I have often noticed people in here asking or chatting about
student use of the Internet. I am intereseted in how best to
supervise student use if they are accessing the Internet on
school equipment during school hours or by a school
subscription from home.

I have found it is very easy of course for anyone to get all
the newsgroups via gopher - how do schools superivse what
students are doing? Should there be supervision? What about
an irate parent storming the principal's office?
```

My problem is that most teachers I have talked to about this do not seem to realise how easy access is to all sorts of areas (including alt. binaries and nasty pictures) and I am worried that worried and twitchy principals may stop any access.

I think some sort of policy/guidelines need to be written to cover schools which allow students access. there is so much excellent curriculum material especially using W W W that I would hate to be limited. I would like to be proactive rather than find myself on the defensive - PLEASE give me some IDEAS!!!?????!!!!!

John:

I recently saw a msg from a user suggesting that each school draw up a Form for each students parents to sign stating that they permitted their child to access the Internet.There could be a rider that the student would agree to abide by some guidelines set up by the school.....

Ben:

That would just discourage students, not prevent them. Generally,you just keep a very close eye on them. To keep students from sending obsene/offensive messages to each other, I wrote up a quick shell script [a computer program] to search mailboxes for a list of words, if it found one, it notified a sysadmin. An addition would be to incorporate this into the sendmail program so that it checks outgoing mail for the list, if it finds a word, it intercepts the message, and passes it to a sysadmin for approval before sending. This of course, put a major strain on the sysadmins, but it may be worth it.

Jane:

YIKES! And place microphones in each classroom, the gym, hallway, and at every desk. If a monitor in the principal's office hears a "word" someone is dipensed pronto to the offending site and the student roundly reprimanded.

What are you teaching by insidiously employing censorship? Do you have ethics and netiquette classes where students can discuss these issues?

What are the rewards for desirable behavior? Or are there only punishments for undesirable behavior?

NOTES

1. This is a World Wide Web (WWW) "address." In this case, it's the address of the NFSNET. WWW browsers such as Internet Explorer and Netscape use these addresses to navigate the Internet. The "http" stands for HyperText Transport Protocol.

   There are several types of WWW addresses:
   http://www.uwm.edu (a WWW address)
   ftp://ftp.cac.washington.edu/pine (an ftp address)
   telnet://alpha2.csd.uwm.edu (a telnet address)
   gopher://gopher.itd.umich.edu:8888 (a Gopher address)

2. The following graph summarizes and also projects the growth of the Internet using the amount of information transferred on the Internet as a measure of this growth. Projections were made using a third-degree polynomial.

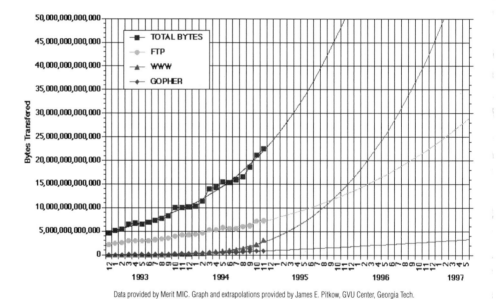

Data provided by Merit MIC. Graph and extrapolations provided by James E. Pitkow, GVU Center, Georgia Tech.

3. See George P. Landow, *Hypertext* (Baltimore: Johns Hopkins University Press, 1992) for a complete discussion of these issues.

4. Vannevar Bush, "As we may think," *Atlantic Monthly 176* (July 1945): 101-8.

5. SPIRE (Spatial Paradigm for Information Retrieval and Exploration) is a software application originally developed for the U.S. intelligence community to analyze large amounts of textual data. Themescape is a part of the SPIRE software that creates a visual landscape from the concepts in the text. For a more detailed explanation, see J. A. Wise et al., "Visualizing the non-visual: Spatial analysis and interaction with information from text documents," *Proceedings of the IEEE Visualization '95* (in press).

6. See Jakob Nielsen, *Multimedia and hypertext: The Internet and beyond* (Mountain View: AP Professional, 1995) for a thorough

history of hypertext applications.

7. These numbers were collected from the NSFNET by Merit NIC Services up until April 1995. Georgia Tech's Graphics and Visualization and Usability Center (http://www.cc.gatech.edu/gvu/stats/NSF/merit.html) was the source of this data.

8. MPEG is a term used to describe a "compressed" movie format, and there are other compression types, such as Apple's QuickTime and Microsoft's Video for Windows. Video on the Internet is usually compressed in one of these formats because otherwise the video file would be extremely large.

   For instance, the 24-second "MARS the Movie" shown here is a 700 kilobyte MPEG file. If the movie was compressed using QuickTime, it expands to over *8 megabytes*, and if "MARS the Movie" were not compressed at all, it could easily swell to over *80 megabytes*!

   MPEG movies can be copied from the Internet to your own personal computer and then viewed. However, special software is required in order for your computer to play back the MPEG movie. Free MPEG player software is available on the Internet for both Windows (e.g., Mpegplay) and the Macintosh (e.g., Sparkle).

9. This former Gopher site was converted to a WWW site in 1997, demonstrating the replacement of older Internet technologies, like Gopher, by WWW browsers.

10. For the full story, see the *Blacklist of Internet Advertisers* (http://math-www.uni-paderborn.de/~axel/BL/blacklist.html#list).

11. Timbuktu Pro software is made by Farallon Computing, Inc., 2470 Mariner Square Loop, Alemeda, CA 94501. (510) 814-5100.

12. In the October 1995 issue of *MacWorld*, the magazine compared the access fees charged by America Online, CompuServe, Delphi, eWorld, GEnie, and Prodigy for "light" (10 hours/month), "moderate" (25 hours/month), and "heavy" (50 hours/month) use. Though the prices charged for light use by all the providers were consistent (~ $25), the fees for moderate and heavy varied drastically. For example, for heavy Internet use, one national provider charged around $90 while another charged over $350.

13. See note 8 above.

14. ISDN, which stands for Integrated Services Digital Network, provides a dial-up Internet connection for home use. It achieves network-type performance by using a special high-speed phone line to provide data transfer rates of between 56 to 128 kilobaud. What makes ISDN desirable is this speed, its increasing availability, and its decreasing price.

15. These e-mail messages have been copied verbatim. Only the authors' names have been changed.

CHAPTER 2 — COMMUNICATING AND EXPLORING FOR INFORMATION ON THE INTERNET

OVERVIEW

This chapter is divided into two major sections (Figure 28):

- The first deals with communicating on the Internet, and the second deals with exploring the Internet for information. The section on communication will focus on using electronic mail, obtaining files from sites on the Internet, and using discussion groups and mailing lists.

- The section on exploring for information will focus on various ways to search and locate information on the Internet and includes a list of useful sites for educators.

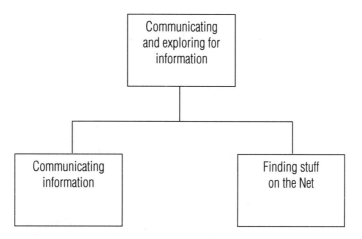

Figure 28: Chapter 2 concept map.

COMMUNICATING INFORMATION

In this section we discuss ways to send and receive information on the Internet. Specifically, we will examine the use of electronic mail (e-mail), file downloads from other computers on the Net, and the use of discussion groups.

E-mail

Electronic mail (e-mail) is the most widely used service of the Internet. Estimates suggest that over one billion e-mail messages are sent on the Internet each month!

Like surface mail, sending communication by e-mail has certain requirements. These include

- something to write with—an e-mail program,
- the address of the sender and the recipient,
- a mechanism to generate and receive messages, and
- a mail delivery system where mail is transported to computers on the Net.

Oh, and by the way, e-mail requires something that is analogous to a postage stamp—a user account from your Internet service provider. Let's briefly explore the function of each of these components.

The e-mail program

E-mail programs come in two varieties—an online mailer and an offline mailer. **Online mailers** (such as the UNIX software Pine and Elm) are programs that deliver, receive, and compose messages on the host computer. Online mailers are like a "dial-up post office" whereby you connect to your service provider, then access the mail program that resides on the provider's computer.

The second type of mail program, **offline mailers** (such as Eudora or the e-mail functions integrated within Communicator or Internet Explorer), are programs that run on a PC or Macintosh and allow you to generate messages before you connect to the host computer. They automatically upload your messages to your host, download mail that is waiting for you on your host computer, and then disconnect so your mail can be viewed at your leisure. Offline mailers are important tools in the classroom. Because they allow students to compose messages within the mail program or on a word processing program before the computer is connected to a host, they will dramatically reduce required online time, and free up access to the computer for other uses. One of the more popular offline mailers, Eudora, is available as freeware on the Internet.

Information about mail programs for Windows and Macintosh and sites where you can download e-mail software can be found on this book's home page.

One type of e-mail program is essentially an "online" system where you compose and read e-mail as you are online to your service provider. These mail programs reside on your service provider's computer. PINE and ELM are examples of these types of programs. These programs have been around a long time and they do not support a mouse. A second type of e-mail program, an "offline" system actually resides on your computer. This type of program allows you to compose and read e-mail messages even though you may not be connected to the Internet. Eudora and the e-mail programs integrated into Netscape's Communicator and Microsoft's Internet Explorer are examples of these types of programs.

In the classroom an offline mailer will be much easier to use, has more features, and will save time, money, and provide greater access for student use. Some of their features will be discussed later on in this section.

The e-mail address

E-mail addresses are a combination of your user name, the @ sign, and the name of your service provider. Your user name or login name is acquired at the time you sign up for an account with the service provider computer you access. The authors' **login** names are hughes and troll1.

The @ sign is used to separate the user name from the service provider (called the **domain**). Tom's domain address at his Internet service provider, ExecPC is execpc.com, while Randall's at the University of Wisconsin-Milwaukee is "csd.uwm.edu". This is the address that our service provider and the university assign to all of their accounts. Note that there are really three elements to the domain address: *uwm*, *csd*, and *edu*. Many universities and companies have more than one large computer connected to the Internet, thus *csd* is a particular computer at the University of Wisconsin-Milwaukee that is connected to the Internet. The *edu* is an Internet suffix signifying the site of a college or university, and *com* is the suffix for commercial sights. Other American suffixes include *org* for nonprofit organizations, *gov* and *mil* for government and military agencies, and *net* for companies or organizations that make use of large networks.

So, putting our user name and the domain name together, we obtain the following e-mail addresses:

user name +	"at sign" +	domain name =	e-mail address
hughes	@	execpc.com	hughes@execpc.com
troll1	@	csd.uwm.edu	troll1@csd.uwm.edu

Table 11: The e-mail address.

Note there are no spaces between the elements of the e-mail address, and although we have used lower case letters, most mailing systems are pretty flexible about case, so generally you won't need to worry about whether you used lower or upper case.

Wondering if someone in the world may share your e-mail address? Since each user on a system has a distinct login and no domains have the same address, each individual on the Internet will have a distinct address.

The mail delivery system

The final requirement of e-mail is the mail delivery program. These programs perform the job of moving e-mail between computers connected to the Internet. Generally they are run on your host computer, so you need not worry about their operation or maintenance. Even though they are invisible to the user, these programs perform such tasks as returning mail to you if the recipient cannot be located, placing your name on messages submitted, maintaining a file of all your mail on the host computer, and allowing you to attach files.

How to write, read, respond to, and save e-mail

In this section we will examine how to write and send an e-mail message, read a message that you have received, respond to a message you have received, and finally we will examine ways that you can save e-mail messages. As we noted previously, e-mail messages, like letters, require addresses. Later on we note several ways to locate e-mail addresses of individuals and groups, but for now let's examine Figures 29, 30, and 31 to send, view, and respond to e-mail using the offline mail program.

Most e-mail programs have the ability to:
- create a new e-mail message (**Send**)
- use some or all of the text from an existing e-mail as part of a new message (**Quote**)
- record commonly used e-mail addresses (**Address**)
- attach text, images, or other types of information to a message (**Attach**)
- spell check e-mail (**Spelling**)
- save a message to a disk file (**Save**)
- add security protection or encryption to an e-mail message (**Security**)

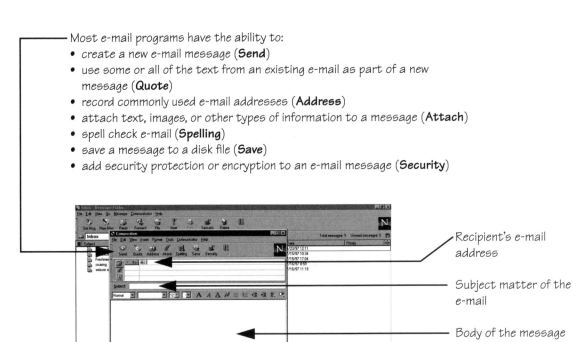

Recipient's e-mail address

Subject matter of the e-mail

Body of the message

Figure 29: Anatomy of an e-mail message.

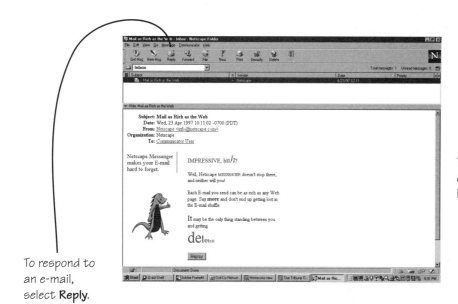

To respond to
an e-mail,
select **Reply**.

This is an example
of what e-mail
looks like.

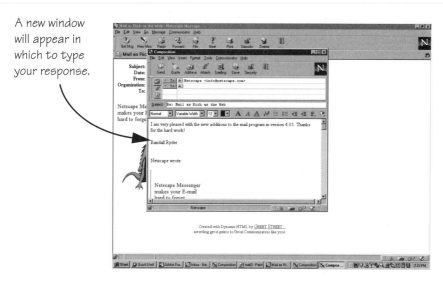

A new window
will appear in
which to type
your response.

Figure 30: Sending an e-mail message.

Saving e-mail and attaching files

There are times when it is useful to remove e-mail messages from your mail program so they can be pasted into a letter, document, or simply be stored on a permanent basis. The process of saving e-mail to a file depends upon whether you are using an online or offline mail program. First, let's examine how to save a message using an online program.

If you use an online program such as Pine, you first need to have the e-mail message on screen. Next you press "E" for export. Pine will then ask you to provide a name for the message. You then press "return" and the message is saved on your service provider's computer. At this point, you will need to exit from Pine and enter your Internet service provider's main menu (how these are

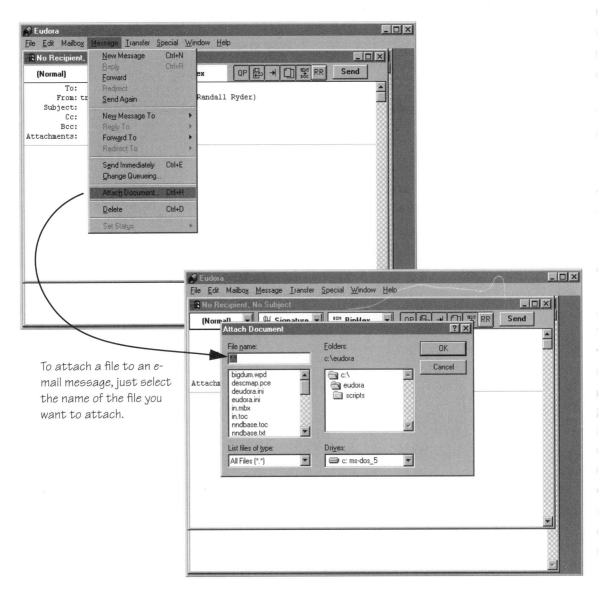

To attach a file to an e-mail message, just select the name of the file you want to attach.

Figure 31: Attaching a file to an e-mail message using Eudora.

accessed and what appears varies among service providers). The file you saved can then be accessed from your system menu. Once this file is brought up and displayed on your screen, you can "copy and paste" it into a word processing program.

To attach documents that exist in a file format, you will first need to place that file on your service provider's computer. Because the process for transferring files varies among service providers, contact them for detailed instructions. Once the file has been transferred to your service provider's computer, if you're using Pine, then the name of that file is entered after the word "Attchmnt".

If you're using an offline e-mail program like Eudora or the e-mail programs in Communicator and Internet Explorer, saving and attaching files is more straightforward. For example, to save a file with Eudora, first enter your word processing program, then access your mail program files in the program's file directory. The file will then automatically be converted into your word processor's file format and will appear on screen. Figure 31 shows how to attach a file to an e-mail message. Another, more direct means of saving a file is to highlight (using your mouse) an e-mail document that is displayed on screen. Next, go to the menu bar at the top of your screen, highlight "Edit," then select "Copy" on the pop-out menu. The document is now on your desktop. Next switch to your word processing program (which can be running in the background), again select "Edit," then "Paste" on the pop-out menu. Your document should now appear before you as a word processing document.

Distribution lists and e-mail filters

There are a number of extremely useful tools contained in most e-mail programs that help organize messages, and make it easier to send messages to groups of people. In what follows we will examine two tools: setting up distribution lists and filtering messages.

Distribution lists

Distribution lists allow you to send a particular e-mail message to a large number of people without entering their individual e-mail addresses. To use a distribution list function you must first create a distribution list. An example of setting up a distribution list for Netscape Communicator is shown in Figure 32. The process is similar for Eudora and Internet Explorer.

The distribution list is a useful tool that will be an invaluable aid in setting up lists for communicating with parents, teachers, and members of professional groups or organizations. Note that you can also add or delete individuals within the list without reentering the entire list.

E-mail filters

A second tool we would like to examine is **filtering**. As you begin to acquire more e-mail messages you will find that it is not unusual to obtain several hundred messages in a given day. Fortunately, the filter tool allows your e-mail program to automatically select messages according to a criteria you select (you can filter based on information from the sender, or text that appears in the subject line or the body of the message), and have those messages placed in a separate mailbox. Then when you read your messages you can go to individual mailboxes that will contain your filtered messages. For example, you may want to set up a mailbox for each of your classes, another mailbox for parents, and yet another for your fellow teachers. An example of how to set up a filter is shown in Figure 33. Complete directions will be found on the help menu of your e-mail program.

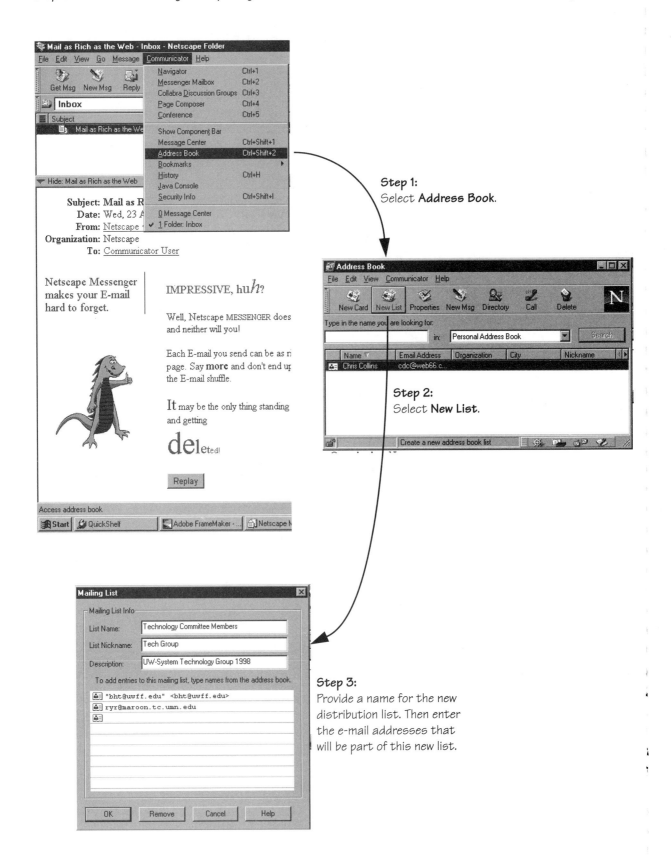

Figure 32: Setting up a distribution list in Netscape Communicator.

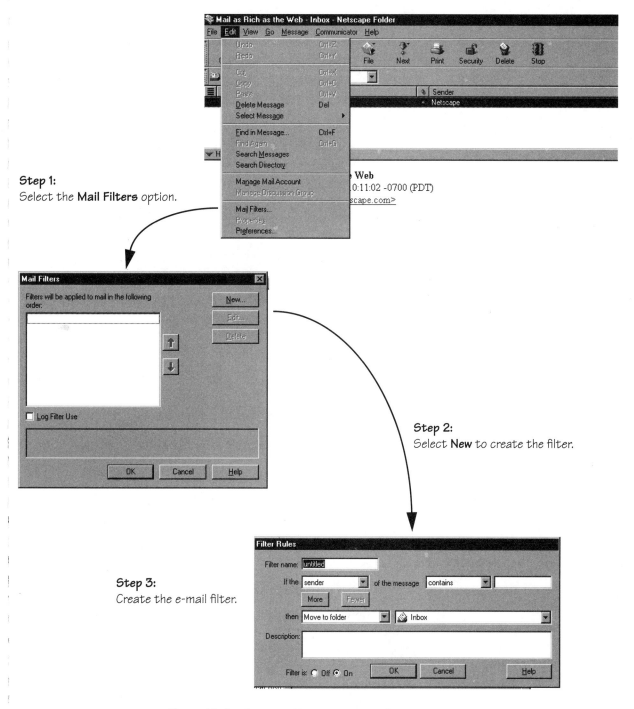

Step 1:
Select the **Mail Filters** option.

Step 2:
Select **New** to create the filter.

Step 3:
Create the e-mail filter.

Figure 33: Setting up a filter in Netscape Communicator.

How to locate e-mail addresses

With so many people on the Net, how do you locate an individual's e-mail address? Whereas on the one hand it is becoming easier to locate people on the Internet, the process is still relatively cumbersome and often involves numerous time-consuming steps. Here are some tips when you are attempting to locate an e-mail address:

- Use a White Page. These are locator services available on the Internet which we have referenced on our Web page

- If an individual is located at a university or governmental agency, connect to their Web site. Individual institutions have their own white pages that are relatively easy to locate and use.

- If you're unable to locate an individual's e-mail address using steps 1 and 2, contact the individual by telephone or surface mail and request his or her e-mail address.

Figure 34: Example of e-mail and White Pages using Bigfoot.

Let's examine how to use the first two steps of this process: using online white pages and connecting to a Web site. Internet white pages are analogous to the telephone white pages. Until recently, there was no single source on the Internet that contained a sizable listing of e-mail addresses. Now, however, services such as B*igfoot* allow one to obtain e-mail and mailing addresses. These services are simple to use and provide a rather extensive, but not exhaustive, listing. An example of locating an e-mail and street listing using Bigfoot is shown in Figure 34.

A cautionary note regarding the use of e-mail locator services. Like telephone numbers, e-mail addresses can be obtained with ingenuity and persistence. However, you should not assume that the recipient of your message is any more obliged to respond to your communication than if you were to send surface mail or place a telephone call to that individual.

For educators this is a particularly important issue. On the surface, it would seem reasonable to assume that e-mail provides ready access to well-known authorities, officials, and personalities. However, you and your students should respect an individual's privacy. As a rule of thumb, if an e-mail address is not listed under a business, governmental agency, or institution, then assume that address is intended for private use.

Using e-mail in the classroom

E-mail can be a flexible and productive classroom tool for the teacher and students. In an educational setting, it can be used as an instructional tool for students, as a communication tool for the teacher, and as a communication tool for the school and the community. In what follows we present suggestions how e-mail can be used by students, how it can serve as a tool for disseminating and gathering information for the teacher, and how it can serve as a direct link between the school and the community.

E-mail provides an inexpensive and immediate means of obtaining and communicating information. Students may use e-mail to communicate with other students in their school or their community, and it can be used as a means of communicating with students on a global basis. For example, a class of students in Denver may be interested in obtaining information on customs in Japanese society. Similarly, these students may be willing to provide information to their Japanese counterparts or engage in some cooperative learning efforts with these students.

But how can the classroom teacher locate an educational colleague in Japan? Fortunately, there are several services that will assist you in establishing intercultural classroom connections. One of these, Intercultural E-mail Classroom Connections (IECC) at St. Olaf College in Minnesota (http://www.stolaf.edu/network/iecc), provides an easy-to-use subscription process allowing teachers to seek partner classrooms for international and crosscultural electronic mail. (Two other ways to locate keypals is by subscribing to the listservs Kidlink or PenPals found in Appendix B.)

Here is an example of a request submitted by Molly Warren in Mt. Prospect, Illinois:

```
Name Molly Warren
Institution Prospect High School (Mt. Prospect,
Illinois)
Subject Social Studies
Students 70 students from three classes
Preference for a partner:
1.  Academic Level  high school students or adults
2.  Country/culture Spain Portugal Canary Islands`
Jamaica Honduras Panama
3.  Language for Lesson  English
4.  Students Needed approximately 705.
Date to Begin  Jan. 10, 1994
Note: I will be beginning a unit on Columbus and his
travels. I am trying to impress upon my students that
Columbus is not viewed the same way by everyone in the
world.  I would like to illustrate this point by having
students "talk" with other students from the places
mentioned above.
```

There are numerous instructional applications of e-mail as a means of linking classrooms on a regional, national, and global basis. Following is an overview of the types of classroom applications we have observed on the Internet. Other e-mail activities can be found in Chapter 3.

In science

- Groups of classrooms located around the world gather information over a two-week period to note the acidity of rainfall. Noting other climatic conditions such as air temperature, humidity, wind speed and direction, and ozone levels (provided by various meteorological sites on the Internet), students generate a global map displaying the levels of acid deposition in rainfall and generate generalizations regarding its distribution and incidence.

- A class of students studying biology establish e-mail links with classrooms dispersed throughout the migratory routes of the American bald eagle and initiate reports on the movement of the eagles during their migration.

- Classrooms in California, Nevada, New Mexico, Oklahoma, Arkansas, Missouri, Illinois, Ohio, West Virginia, and New York establish a weather observation link to track the movement, development, and effect of a low pressure system. With the assistance of infrared images, visible satellite images (obtained from the Internet), and their recordings of temperature, humidity, wind speed, precipitation, and barometric pressure, the students observe the effects of the low pressure system. Then they predict its effects on various parts of the country, submitting their information via e-mail to their participating sites throughout the country.

In math

- Classes in selected cities throughout the country conduct a poll to determine the population's views on national issues such as gun control, the support for a female presidential candidate, and a national ban on smoking in all public places. Each site exchanges collected data, and an analysis of findings is conducted and shared among the participating schools.

- Three schools in the mid-Atlantic states engage in a simulated cross-country gymkhana. Students begin the competition at the same location with different "assigned automobiles" and are provided $2000.00 in script cash. The students must plot their route, calculate expenses, and determine road construction, weather conditions, and overnight stays by contact sites along their route. Each day during the competition, participants gather information on the Internet and submit their daily travel plans and expenses to a host class that keeps records of time, expenses, and along-the-route comments.

In English

- In California, a grade school posts an announcement of a poetry contest on various Usenet bulletin boards. Students around the country submit various types of poems to the school, which then routes the poems to a group of high school students at a fine arts specialty high school in Minneapolis who serve as judges in the contest.

- In Cleveland, Ohio, a high school class locates peer classes in England, Germany, Portugal, Scotland, and South Africa to write a generative short story dealing with a fictitious global community established to train a cadre of individuals for travel to and settlement of a distant planet. Each portion of the story is written by a different group of students who then communicate their portion to their peers by e-mail.

As you can see from these examples, there are a myriad of instructional applications for e-mail. Whereas each application must be tailored to the needs of the students, the objectives of the teacher, and the available instructional time, the following are some uses of e-mail in the school setting that can be applied to various subject matter content or grade levels. Note that some of these applications require students to have individual e-mail addresses. Obtain these by contacting your service provider.

Cross-curricular application

- Peer Writing Evaluation—Using various forms of peer evaluation instruments, students can exchange written works for feedback from each other. This can occur within a class from remote locations or between classrooms. Word processing documents can be "dropped" into e-mail by pasting the document from the word processing program into a mail program. Simply highlight the piece of writing in your word processor file, then "copy" the file to your clipboard. The file will remain in your computer's memory. Now execute the mail program, enter the "edit" command at the top of your screen, and "paste" the document in your mail program.

- Homework Line—You can set up a distribution list on your mail program so that a single message can be sent to various e-mail addresses automatically. This is a useful way to set up a homework line, where homework assignments can be accessed from a home computer.

- Community Network—Community members can make use of e-mail to act as tutors for students, to serve as reviewers of students' writing projects and to obtain information on school news or events. A relatively new group of individuals to become active in the use of the Internet is retired citizens. These members of the community can provide a useful role in mentoring students, serving as vocational resources and tutors.

- Parent Newsletter—With computers being present in approximately 50% of all homes, e-mail can be a useful means to provide parents with up-to-date information about projects, activities, and school and classroom news and events.

- Parent-Teacher Communication—Teachers and parents are often difficult to locate during the workday due to their busy schedules. E-mail provides a convenient mechanism for personal communication between teachers and parents. We have found that often the time involved in telephoning between parents and teachers exceeds that necessary to compose and send an e-mail message.

- Communicate with Public Officials—Most elected officials at the state, national, and in many cases local level have e-mail addresses. For class activities involved in communicating with these officials, e-mail provides a rapid means of communication.

These are just a few of the educational applications of e-mail. Many useful ideas on classroom activities can be obtained from the K-12 instructional resource list found on our home page. The success of using e-mail in the classroom setting requires that certain guidelines be followed in planning, administering, and devoting resources.

Here is a summary of what teachers participating in an online discussion sponsored by IECC found to be useful in their applications of e-mail:

- Adequate Time—E-mail use should not be just another add-on to the normal curriculum. An honest commitment requires students and teachers to allocate an appropriate amount of time.

- Adequate Access to Resources—Resources must work, be reasonably close by, and be reasonably understandable for successful e-mail classroom connections.

- Pedagogical Leadership—Teachers must strive to exert leadership to ensure that e-mail connections are used with civility and a sense of dignity for all participants. This requires information for students on how to act on the Net, requirements for student behavior and performance, maintenance with early and continuous personal and professional contact with partner teachers, and a proactive encouragement to students to assume ownership of the leadership, administration, organization, and evaluation of activities involving e-mail.

> **Teacher comments on using e-mail**
>
> **From Juan, a 4th grade teacher in Texas:** *Generally my students use e-mail to correspond with other students around the world. We get in touch with these students through a locator service. I guess the students like communicating with other students, but we have had problems getting the students in other countries to respond because they don't have the ease of access we do. I found that you can't expect answers very quickly to your messages.*
>
> **From Alicia, an 11th grade teacher in Georgia:** *My students use e-mail primarily to communicate with other students throughout the state on a history project we are working on. I find that things move a lot more smoothly when students have individual [e-mail] mailboxes on my account. That way I can keep track of their communications and have a well-designed system to maintain the messages and store them. Our biggest problem is finding time to compose messages so we tend to have students write their messages using a word processor, then they can bring the file to class and we insert it as an attachment in the e-mail message. This has saved a lot of time and allows students the opportunity to use the spell/grammar checker.*

Listserv

Our discussion of e-mail assumed you were communicating with specific individuals and you possess these individuals' e-mail addresses. There is another use of e-mail that is not specific to a person but rather to a group of individuals who share a common interest. These are called listservs or mailing lists.

Listserv is an automated form of e-mail where a computer program distributes e-mail to individuals who have placed their names on a mailing list. This is analogous to a carbon copy function when mailing a letter, or subscribing to a surface mail newsletter. With listserv everyone who subscribes to the mailing list receives a copy of all articles submitted by members of the mailing list. These articles are routed to all subscribers automatically by a mailing list server.

The concept of a server receiving an article, then mailing it to everyone on a list (termed "mail explosion") may result in the article being sent to thousands of individuals who subscribe to the listserv. Notice that once you belong to a mailing list, you receive all postings of the group. If you belong to just a few mailing lists, you may find literally hundreds of articles each day in your e-mail box. So it is important that you select your group(s) wisely and be prepared to receive a lot of mail!

Listservs are contacted through your e-mail software program. The first step in using a listserv is to locate one that may be of interest to you. You will find names of education listservs in Appendix B. A complete listing of all listservs can be obtained from our Web site.

Signing up for a mailing list requires submitting an e-mail message to the mailing list server indicating you wish to be placed on the mailing list. To subscribe to a mailing list, an e-mail message is submitted to the listserv address. The subject, or RE:, is left blank. In the message simply write "SUBSCRIBE," the NAME OF THE LISTSERV, and your NAME.

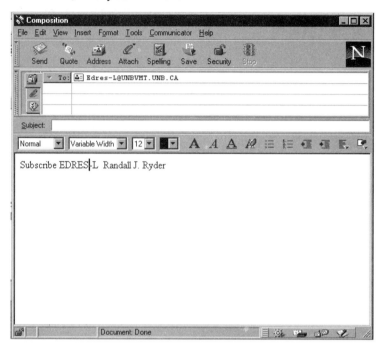

Figure 35: Subscribing to a listserv.

Figure 35 is an example of a message used to subscribe to the mailing list EDRESL, which provides information on educational resources on the Internet. To be removed from a mailing list, simply follow the same procedure for subscribing, except insert the text "UNSUBSCRIBE" in the message.

Because there are so many mailing lists available, and the process to subscribe and unsubscribe is so painless, you may consider subscription to one or two lists for a week then unsubscribe and sign up for another list or two. This way you will gain a sense of the content of various mailing lists as well as the process of using this form of e-mail.

Usenet discussion groups

Usenet is a collection of computers that act like electronic bulletin boards where individuals post, read, and reply to messages focusing on specific areas of interest. These electronic bulletin boards are commonly referred to as **newsgroups** although most of them don't contain "news" of current events.

At present there are over 30,000 of these electronic newsgroups available on the Net. Each one is dedicated to a specific topic.

Obviously with so many newsgroups, the content they address runs the gamut from the pious to the pornographic.

In what follows we will provide a brief description of how newsgroups work, how you can locate and subscribe to newsgroups, and finally we will discuss newsgroup etiquette.

How does Usenet work?

Usenet is a large collection of computers scattered throughout the world that allows users to share information with each other. Generally, the content of this information is similar to e-mail but is transmitted and stored by programs distinct from the electronic mailers, and the messages on Usenet are public rather than private or personal communications.

You may consider this to be a form of an electronic parlor, neighborhood coffee house, or a revitalization of the concept of a social club. Each computer on Usenet maintains a set of messages called "articles" that are maintained by a news administrator. This individual is responsible for maintaining the software to run the newsgroup, monitors disk space, and deletes old messages.

Additionally, some newsgroups are *moderated*. In this case, an individual approves of the articles before they can be posted, posts articles of note to the newsgroup, and may respond to individuals with personal communications via e-mail.

Most newsgroups, however, are *unmoderated*. Quite simply, this means that everything that is submitted is posted regardless of its content.

Locating and observing newsgroups

Locating newsgroups is a relatively straightforward task. With a little understanding of how the groups are categorized, located, and accessed, you will find yourself immersed in a wealth of interesting and enlightening resources.

Discussion groups are categorized into the following seven primary hierarchies:

- comp—Discussions of computer software and hardware. Examples: *comp.virus*—a group addressing common computer viruses and their detection. *comp.windows.misc*—applications and comments related to the use of Microsoft Windows.

- misc—You guessed it . . . discussions that don't fit anywhere else. This category includes education. Examples: *misc.writing*—discussions dealing with various forms of writing. *misc.fitness*—discussions dealing with individuals' interests in various fitness programs and suggestions for training.

- news—Discussions of Usenet News such as news policy, new newsgroups. Examples: *news.future*—a group devoted to future applications of technology. *news.announce*—a nifty way to draw attention to conferences on various topics.

- rec—Discussions dealing with recreational topics such as

sports, hobbies, movies, travel, and so on. Examples: *rec.folkdancing*—discussions related to various forms of folk dancing and groups devoted to folk dancing. *rec.rollercoaster*—aficionados of roller coasters discuss their most thrilling moments and rides.

- sci—Discussions dealing with science-related topics such as biology, physics, and astronomy. Examples: *sci.military*—individuals interested in various aspects of military science. *sci.med.nutrition*—discussion on various principles and theories related to human nutrition.

- soc—Discussions related to social and cultural issues such as religion, philosophy, anthropology, sociology, and ethnicity. Examples: *soc.religion.quaker*—a group devoted to discussion of various aspects of the Quaker religion. *soc.culture.japan*—Discussions regarding Japanese culture.

- talk—These are discussion groups on controversial topics dealing with a wide variety of issues such as drugs, crime, pollution, right and left wing ideology, and so on. Examples: *talk.politics.soviet*—discussions of politics and political events occurring in Russia. *talk.rumors*—the posting and discussion of rumors.

Discussion groups are accessed and controlled by your Internet service provider. And there may be certain restrictions on the discussion groups you can access. For listings of specific discussion groups within the categories above, simply connect to your service provider using your Web browser program. Next, select your discussion groups reader function within your browser. If you use Internet Explorer, activate the news function by going to the menu bar at the top of your screen and click on "mail". From the drop-down menu that appears, select "read news". If you use Netscape Communicator, go to the menu bar at the top of your screen, select "Communicator," then select "Collabra Discussion Group" that appears on the drop down menu. And if you use a version of Netscape Navigator, go to the menu bar at the top of the screen, select "Window", then "Netscape News" from the drop-down menu. Once your newsreader appears on screen, select discussion groups. Your program will then download all discussion groups that can be accessed by your service provider. This may take several minutes. Once the discussion groups appear on screen you will need to subscribe to those you are interested in using. To subscribe, simply highlight the discussion groups, then click on the "Subscribe" button in your newsreader. Once you have subscribed, the discussion groups will automatically appear in your newsreader.

Figure 36 provides an example of the newsgroup browser listings under k12. Now you are ready to look at the listings under a particular newsgroup. Simply move the cursor to any of the articles listed, then click on it with your mouse. Your newsreader will then

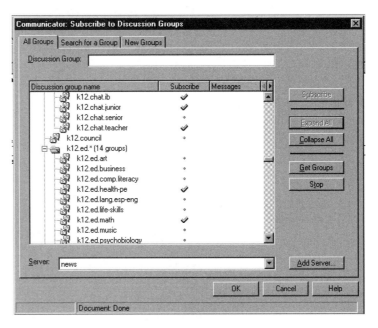

Figure 36: K12 discussion groups.

display the recent listings for the newsgroup.

Let's examine the anatomy of article listings under k12.ed.comp.literacy. (See Figure 37.) You will note that this article is actually a response to a previous article in which the respondent inserted the original message. In this example, it is obvious that

The news program compiled this information.

This was the original message posted by Jim.

This is Bill's response to Jim's posting. Note that it is a useful message for all newsgroup members.

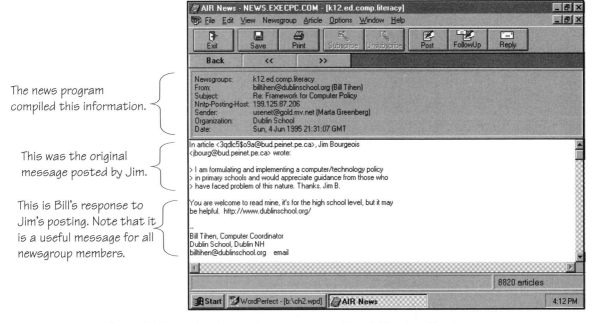

Figure 37: Example of a newsgroup message from k12.comp.literacy.

this article is useful to various discussion group members as it directs them to resources that are likely to be of general interest.

If you would like to begin your tour of discussion groups with those dealing with education, a partial listing of groups dedicated to education can be found in Appendix B.

What do you do once you are connected to a discussion group?

You may note at the top of the menu several options available to the user. Whereas the screens of various news software readers may be somewhat different, most will allow you to take the perspective of a recipient and a responder.

As a recipient you can read the article on screen, save an article to disk, or you can print the article on your printer. In either case, to copy the article you simply click on the button to "print" or "save to disk" and, voila, you have a copy.

As a responder you may either (1) reply to the message via personal e-mail, (2) follow up with a reply to an article (which will then be posted on the discussion group), or (3) post a new message on the newsgroup. The option you select depends upon your purpose, who you would like to read your message, and discussion group netiquette.

If you wish to direct a personal, private communication in response to the article, then submit an e-mail response to the individual. Note that many articles are posted by individuals seeking personal advice, support, or resources.

In general, personal requests demand a personal response. For example, if a teacher in Oregon is asking for the name of a good science software program to teach some of the concepts of heredity, then it is appropriate to respond with a personal e-mail message. However, if that same teacher posts an article addressing his or her views on the teaching of heredity, then your response should be posted to the newsgroup readers. After all, discussion groups are designed to stimulate thought, promote dialogue, and facilitate the exchange of ideas in an open forum.

If your purpose is to respond to a specific article, and your response is intended for the discussion group participants, then you will want to follow up on the article so your response will be available for all to see. If you wish to initiate a new idea or inquiry for all discussion group participants to read and possibly react to, then you will want to post a new article.

Creating your own discussion group

Discussion groups can be a powerful tool in the classroom to promote student discussions and to allow students the opportunity to interact with others. There are several ways for you to establish your own discussion group for your students, the community, or your staff. The most expeditious route is to create a discussion group for your home page. Discussion groups can readily be created in most of the leading Web authoring tools. For example, Microsoft's FrontPage allows you to create a discussion group in a matter of minutes! Once created, the discussion group becomes a part of your home page rather than being accessible from a discussion groups reader.

A second option for creating a discussion group is to have your service provider generate a discussion group listing under its domain name. These discussion groups can then be accessed by anyone having an Internet connection. We, for example, use discussion groups for the classes we teach at the university and require our students to engage in topical discussions at least once a week. These discussion groups reside on our university server and can be accessed by anyone having Internet access. The advantage of this system is its ability to allow us to engage students and professors at other academic institutions in our discussions. For more information on establishing this type of discussion group contact your Internet service provider.

Here are some examples of classroom activities that have involved the use of discussion groups.

- *Community Crisis Line*. A school district in New York state sets up a moderated discussion group to deal with a tragic traffic accident that resulted in the deaths of several high school students. Parents, students, and counselors from the community engage in a dialog about the tragedy and the problem of teenage drinking. This discussion group continued throughout the year and broadened into a variety of social issues in the community.

- *Intercultural Discussions*. An elementary school in South Carolina sets up a discussion group that includes students in Europe and South America to determine views toward education, politicians, and taxation to support public works and social agencies. As a culminating activity, the students engage in creating a society that reflects the views of a worldwide culture.

- *Vocational Assistance*. A school district in California establishes a school-to-work discussion group that focuses on careers. As students examine different career opportunities, they engage in discussions with their peers and members of various trades and professional groups to gain a better understanding of job opportunities. As a result of this discussion group, various summer internship programs are established throughout the community to provide students on-the-job experience. At the same time, business groups meet to discuss with educators some of their impressions of students' views toward the educational process.

While the educational applications of discussion groups can be a powerful tool to promote students' knowledge, their use has been somewhat limited in classroom situations. We encourage you, therefore, to create a discussion group and explore its applications to your classroom and the community.

Usenet netiquette

Usenet provides the potential for an enlightening environment where teachers exchange ideas, discuss current topics in education, and obtain various information on curriculum, instruction, and the use of technology. Used properly, educational discussion groups have the potential to provide the means for unlimited staff development.

To ensure the integrity and quality of these discussion groups, it is important that users recognize their obligation to follow certain accepted behaviors.

The following guidelines should be examined carefully and applied as you engage in discussion groups.

1. *Be Kind to Your Audience*. Remember, written discourse tends to allow many more interpretations than face-to-face communication. While there is a tendency to be wowed by the technology of the Net, remember that the recipients of your postings are humans with feelings, beliefs, and values that vary from yours.

2. *Tailor Your Communication to Your Audience.* With any good communication, consider whom you are posting to and tailor your language and message to the audience.

3. *Make it Short and Specific*. Postings should be brief, no more than approximately 80 words in length. If you have a lengthy document, place it in a mailbox on your service provider's mail system, then post its availability to discussion group members.

4. *Don't Participate in Inappropriate Postings, Bizarre Behavior, or Off-the-Subject Remarks*. Restrain yourself. Some citizens of the Net (or "Netizens") make it a habit of submitting abusive or personal attacks against the poster of a message. This behavior, called flaming, can be intimidating for those who are becoming acquainted with e-mail and Usenet. The best defense to this sort of behavior is to ignore it! Another annoyance is the posting of messages, normally for the purpose of marketing a product or service, to large numbers of discussion groups. This behavior, called spamming, normally leads to the removal of the message rather readily by discussion group moderators, or to members of the discussion group deluging the initiator of the posting with e-mail messages requesting that he or she cease submitting spammed messages.

5. *Never, Ever Allow Students to Provide Their Complete Name, Their Phone Number, or Their Address*. Regrettably, there have been cases of individuals lurking in discussions groups with the intent of initiating malicious, perverse, or illegal behaviors. Don't allow your students or yourself to become victims of these individuals. If you feel you would like to contact individuals you have met through discussion groups, rely upon school addresses and telephone numbers. And in the event that you or your students are approached on the Usenet by individuals who may have an ulterior motive, contact your service provider

immediately. Unfortunately, the Internet can be used by unscrupulous individuals. Be Net smart!

6. *Don't Post Personal Replies.* Discussion groups are intended as a forum for public discussion and information. If you would like to respond with a personal message, use e-mail. And when posting a question to the discussion group, ask that responses be directed to you personally via e-mail.

7. *Provide an Article Reference.* Because newsgroup articles reside on your service provider's computers, what may have been the previous posting on your screen will not necessarily be in the same order on the screen of a user with a different service provider. Thus it is important not to refer to a posting as "the previous message." Always identify the title, author, and date of the posting when providing a follow-up.

Receiving files

In this section we discuss ways to locate and transfer files from the Internet. Surprisingly, many individuals are unfamiliar with the hundreds of thousands of files that can be downloaded from the Internet to their computers. These files may contain text, graphics, sound, video clips, or they may be shareware or freeware software programs that will run on a variety of computers. Indeed, as we noted in Chapter 1, most of the software required to connect your school or personal computer to the Internet can be obtained online, as can books, articles, and mailing lists that describe the use of the various Internet tools.

In what follows, we provide a brief overview of the steps to locate and download files to your computer, then describe some of the educational applications of this process.

Locating and downloading files

Until recently, obtaining files on the Internet required knowledge of UNIX computer language to navigate through **ftp** (which stands for file transfer protocol), which was a standard tool for moving files from one computer to another. This was a rather tedious and cumbersome process. And frankly, most Internet beginners found it confusing, frustrating, and downright nasty.

Not to worry though. Along came the Web that transformed the process into a simple routine of Connect, Click, and Grab. Let's examine this three-step routine to demonstrate how you can obtain files. Basically, the first step involves locating a site that maintains files that you can transfer to your computer. Later on in this section, we will discuss ways to locate files.

For the time being, let's assume that you have been given the **URL** (i.e., Uniform Resource Locator) address (http://www.wws.princeton.edu/~ota/ns20/pubs_f.html) a site at Princeton University that serves as a repository for the publications generated by the former Office of Technology Assessment.

Following are the steps in obtaining files from this site.

Step one: Connect

Connecting to the site is an easy task. Simply enter the address and your browser will locate the host computer and respective file you have requested (Figure 38).

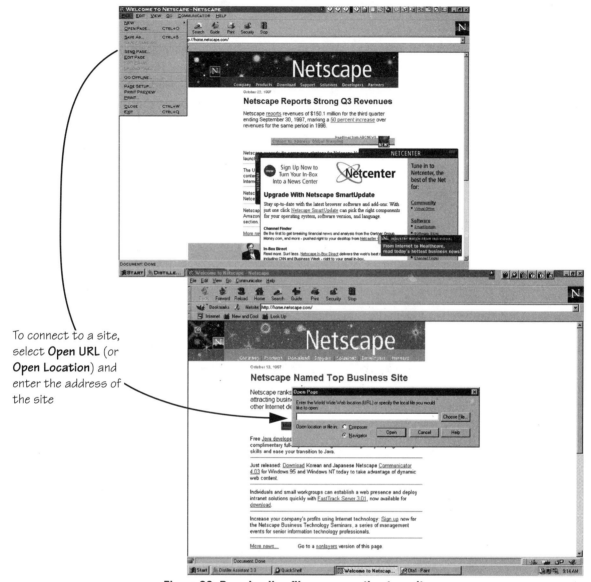

To connect to a site, select **Open URL** (or **Open Location**) and enter the address of the site

Figure 38: Downloading files—connecting to a site.

Step two: Click

Note that under the heading OTA *Publications,* we see an item labeled *Teachers and Technology: Making the Connection.* This is a file that can be downloaded to your computer. The process to initiate a download is described in Figure 39.

Step three: Grab

Note that *Communicator* is informing us that an undetermined file is coming our way, and prompts us to where we would like to save it. (Figure 39).

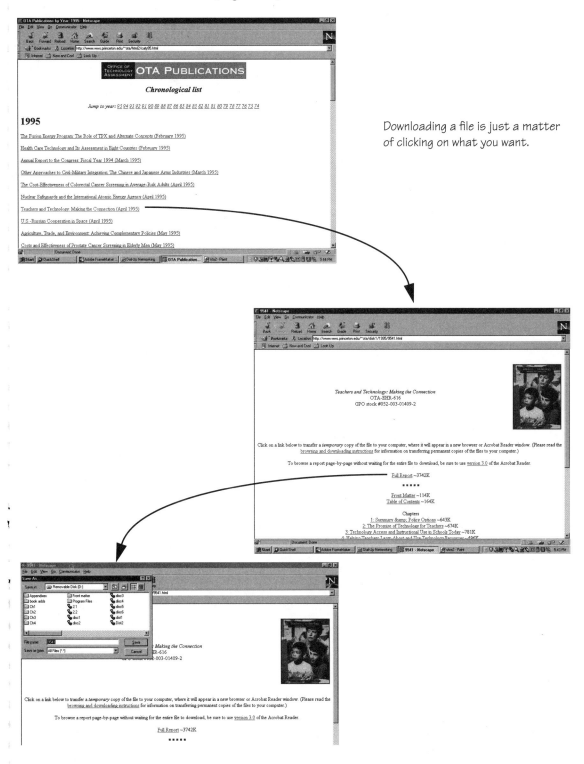

Downloading a file is just a matter of clicking on what you want.

Figure 39: Downloading a file—selecting a file.

At this point we have the option of either saving the file to a hard drive (in this case C or D) or to a diskette drive (A or B) where it will be written to a diskette. Because the size of files to be downloaded is not always indicated at the site where you located a file, it is a good idea to place the file on your hard drive (if you have a lot of unused space). Otherwise, you may find that your fixed disk will become full and your downloading operation will terminate.

With a little experience, you will quickly become proficient in downloading various types of files. And, frankly, you will be amazed at the magnitude of files that are available on the Internet. A sort of digital candy store awaits you!

Unfortunately, file acquisition in an educational setting can present a few obstacles. Generally, these obstacles relate to (1) time required to download a file and (2) file management. Depending upon the number of computers you have connected to the Internet, downloading time can become a rather crucial issue in the classroom. Depending on the speed of your Internet connection, some files can take an hour or more to download.

If your school or classroom has limited access, tying up your connection for long periods of time while students are present in order to obtain a file on the Net may be impractical. In this case, consider establishing a school policy for downloading files. Also you may find it useful to restrict access to early morning or evening hours, dedicate a computer to file downloads, or if resources allow, designate an individual who will assume the responsibility of procuring files.

A second obstacle you may encounter is managing files. Whereas the Internet is a rich source of information, sometimes just managing this information can be a problem. Restrictions imposed by space on your hard drive, keeping track of disks, and maintaining a file archive can become tedious. Consider using a schoolwide database whereby teachers can enter the files they have acquired. This information may include the title of the file, its intended use (content, grade level), comments regarding its use, and where the file can be located. Centralizing your school's collection will provide access for the entire faculty.

Finding files to download

We have found three procedures useful in locating files to transfer from a computer on the Internet to your personal computer. One involves the use of sites that contain thousands of software programs, a second is the use of search engines, and a third procedure to locate files is access to Usenet.

Software sites

There are a number of Web sites that contain hundreds, even thousands of software programs that can be transferred to your computer. Some of these programs are freeware (free software) and some of them are shareware (programs for which you pay the author of the program a nominal fee after you have had the opportunity to evaluate it). Three Web sites that are dedicated to downloading files that we have found easy to use, provide their own search engines for locating software, and that update are The Jumbo (*www.jumbo.com*), SHAREWARE.COM (*www.shareware.com*), and ZDNet *Software Library* (*www.hotfiles.com*).

WWW search engines

A second way to locate files to download is the use of the WWW "search engines," which are Web sites that contain searchable databases. A complete description of the various search engines and their use can be found in the next major section in this chapter, so we will limit our discussion here to their use in locating files.

Locating software on a search engine is effortless. First, you connect with a search engine, enter the name or type of files you are attempting to locate, then browse the responses that are provided by the search. The results of a search for chemistry software using the MetaCrawler search engine are shown in Figure 40.

Figure 40: Using a search engine.

Although WWW search engines simplify locating and downloading files, they were not designed exclusively for that purpose. So don't assume that the results of your search will routinely identify accessible files.

Many files obtained over the Internet are *compressed* to reduce the amount of space they use. Once you have downloaded these files to your computer, a decompression utility must be used to decode (or uncompress) them. Decompression files for Macintosh and PC computers can be downloaded from Jumbo (http://www.jumbo.com) which, by the way, contains over 20,000 software programs!

Discussion groups

Usenet discussion groups provide a valuable reference for teachers seeking assistance in locating files on the Internet. Posting an article requesting assistance to locate a file not only provides a location for that file, but it is likely to provide commentary from colleagues who have had the opportunity to use that file in the classroom. You will find the K-12 groups referenced earlier in this chapter to be a good starting point for your postings.

Here are some useful tips for seeking assistance in locating files through discussion group postings:

- *State the nature of the file you are seeking, the type of computer operating system you are using, and a brief description of how you intend to use the file*. The more specific your description, the more likely you are to receive responses suitable to your inquiry. Also remember that many files cannot be used for both Windows and Macintosh, so it is useful to state the operating system you use.

- *Request assistance for the addresses of WWW or Gopher sites that may contain curricular materials, computer programs, text, and graphic files for the topic or content you are seeking.* You would be amazed at the useful files we have come across by browsing through sites that have been referred to us by our students and colleagues. Although you may not find that file you need at the moment, you're certain to come across numerous gems that can be used in the future.

- *Post articles on discussion groups used by individuals who may specialize in the information you are seeking.* You're likely to get considerable assistance from the experts, aficionados, and hobbyists who frequent discussion groups. A teacher seeking graphic files of photos taken from the shuttle program, for example, could post a message on *sci.space.shuttle* or *sci.space*.

- *Specify in the subject of your posting "Teachers Seeking Assistance."* This will signal to users that your posting does not address an ongoing topic being addressed by the group. Be specific in your request, note that you are an educator, and that you are requesting this information for educational purposes. And make certain that you provide an e-mail address where you would like responses submitted.

You may find that other teachers have had the opportunity to use the desired files with their students. Often they may provide suggestions for alternatives based on the intended use. For example, we recently came across a posting requesting a particular freeware program for basic mathematics. One respondent indicated that he had used the software, found it too difficult for students, and suggested two alternatives that he had found quite effective with his students. We followed up with an e-mail message to the teacher who had originated the posting several months after reading the posting on the *k12.math* group. Here, in part, are some of her observations.

> I frequently use this discussion group for advice from teachers who have used different software programs. Recently I have been interested in examining some of the programs (files) that can be downloaded on the Internet. My request for information on math software really paid off as I received a number of useful suggestions as to where I could find programs on the Net as well as comments from people who had used them in their classroom. You asked in your message whether I had tried the software that was suggested on the *k12.math* discussion group. Thanks to the feedback I received I actually found some programs that are better than the one I was attempting to locate. Using the discussion group saved me time, provided a nice outlet for exchanging some ideas with my peers, and helped our school obtain some useful software. This is particularly helpful with our very tight budget! (Theresa, a 4th grade teacher in Ohio.)

In summarizing our discussion of downloading files, we would like to emphasize the potential this medium presents to teachers. With relatively little investment in time, and at little or no cost, rich resources can be obtained readily for classroom instruction. Additionally, new software and files become available each day so it is important that if you don't find what you need upon your first inquiry you may want to try again in a few weeks.

FINDING STUFF ON THE NET

In this final section of the chapter, we address ways to locate information on the Net. This discussion will focus on two resources: **search engines** and Web sites that contain a variety of resources that are likely to be used by educators. As usual we will direct you to links on our home page that will provide you with hands-on experiences, and we will provide suggestions for the applications of these resources in the classroom.

Search engines

Search engines are sites on the Net that will seek information anywhere on the Internet. These search programs don't actually search through the Internet, rather they search through a database of locator addresses and descriptors of the information located at various Gopher, WWW, and Telnet sites.

Some of these search engines have rather exhaustive lists of locator addresses, so your chances of locating information that exists on the Net are quite good. Not all of them are kept as up to date as others, some tend to be rather slow compared to their available counterparts, and, most importantly, if you conduct a search on the same topic using a number of these search engines, your results will vary widely.

Some of the more widely used sites include Yahoo (http://www.yahoo.com), Lycos (http://www.lycos.com/), WebCrawler (http://webcrawler.com), InfoSeek (http://www.infoseek.com/Home?pg=Home.html&sv=N4&svx=logo), AltaVista (http://altavista.digital.com) and MetaCrawler (http://www.metacrawler.com).

Although the format for entering information is quite similar, the words or phrases used as descriptors will vary somewhat. It is important to read the online instructions. For example, some search engines conduct a Boolean search—meaning that when using two words, the words will always be linked together. Thus when searching for *writing assessment*, only information that contains both the words *writing* and *assessment* would be provided. The Boolean connectors allow the search to be more precise and they will tend to reduce unrelated information.

Note the process of conducting a search on AltaVista for the term "cooperative learning". The results of this search produced over 9,000 "hits" or possible sites that contain information on cooperative learning. The search provides a listing for each hit that includes a brief description of the content of the site and the Web address of the site. Here, for example, is one of the sites presented in the search results:

Cooperative Learning

COOPERATIVE LEARNING. To facilitate the integrated theme, each academic team has classrooms with movable walls. This structural design maximizes the... http://www.coedu.usf.edu/~campbell/images/cooperative.html - size 2K - 12.Mar.96 - English

Unfortunately, not all of the sites identified by AltaVista were relevant to our search on cooperative learning.

As we noted, the search on "cooperative learning" resulted in over 9,000 hits when using the AltaVista search engine. However, when we conducted an identical search on WebCrawler we obtained 327 hits. While it would be tempting to suggest that one

Galaxy (© 1995 TradeWave Corp.)

Lycos (© 1995 Lycos, Inc.)

Magellan

WWW Catalog

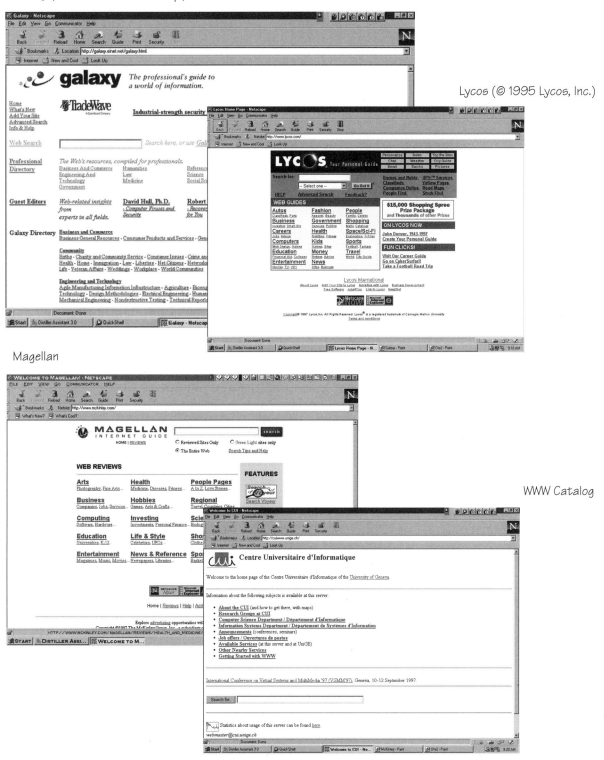

Figure 41: Internet search engines (part 1).

WWW Worm (© 1995 Oliver A. McBryan, University of Colorado)

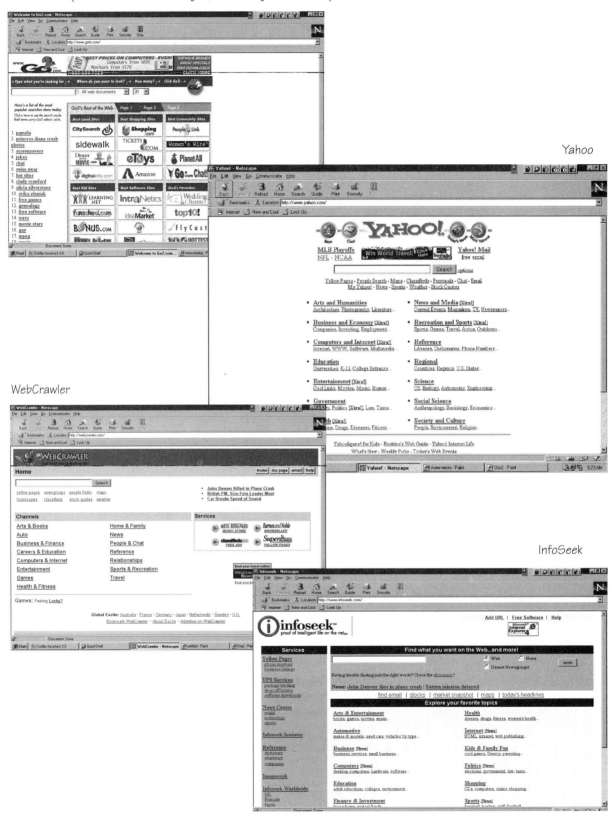

Yahoo

WebCrawler

InfoSeek

Figure 42: Internet search engines (part 2).

search engine is more robust in its efforts to find information, it really depends on the type of information you are searching for. And what may seem to be a powerful engine for one search may produce rather scant results on another. So what does one do? How about using a number of search engines all at once? Yup, there is such a tool available to you. One of these, MetaCrawler (http://www.metacrawler.com), simultaneously conducts a search using the databases of five other search engines, then compiles and presents the results (Figure 40). In other words, MetaCrawler is a "search engine of search engines." Surprisingly, this process takes no longer than conducting a search on the individual search engines, and obviously the results are rather comprehensive. We have found that MetaCrawler provides us with the most comprehensive results, and for that reason it is our search engine of choice.

There is one more source for search engines that we would like to mention. Actually it is a web site that allows you to search over 120 different kinds of search engines and databases. It is called the All-in-One Search Page (http://www.albany.net/allinone/all1www.html#WWW). This site actually presents the name of a search engine or database and a window to enter your search information. Once entered, you then click a button and the search is conducted from the All-in-One site. An example of the format of this page can be seen in Figure 43. This is a gem of a site and one which you should bookmark and make available to your students.

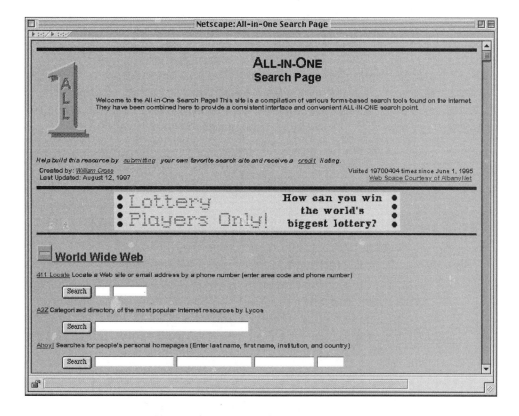

Figure 43: The All-in-One search engine.

Tips when using search engines

Search engines provide a useful and powerful tool for locating information on the Internet. As we have seen from the previous examples, the product of a search may produce unrelated information, and it may present a rather limited description of the content that can be located at the site listed. We have also noted that different search engines will produce different results on the same query. Recognizing these observations and the fact that it would be difficult to maintain a database that would account for the thousands of entries and deletions that occur to information on the Internet each day, consider the following three steps when using searchable databases:

1. Have your query proceed from the very specific to the more general. If you are looking for information on concepts of curricular reform in schools, it is best to begin with a query like "school curricular reform" or "educational curricular reform." In the event that the query produces few results, then proceed to the more general phrase "educational reform" or "school reform." Although you are likely to obtain fewer relevant sources in the second example, it is important to note that these search engines examine descriptors of the information source in seeking links. If certain key words are omitted when describing the original document, then it's likely that the document will not be located in the search.

2. Limit the number of "hits" you want displayed. Limiting the number of hits you accept in your search will take less time. Remember that it takes time to conduct the search, but it also takes considerable time to examine each of the hyperlinked sites that will be referenced in the search results. Chances are that ten to twenty sources will be adequate. If not, return to the search engine and increase the allowable hits.

3. If results are not satisfactory, use multiple search engines. As we have noted, different engines produce different results. If you obtain unsatisfactory results, don't assume that the information does not exist on the Net. Consider using several engines for each search. And remember, a particular engine will not consistently produce the most rewarding results.

Search agents and intelligent tools

As good as search engines are in locating information, there two new products available to provide educators even more powerful ways to locate information. One of these is called an intelligent search tool. It is similar to the MetaCrawler search engine in that it will search using a variety of different search engines, but it also provides a detailed summary of the content of the site (including the number of links and graphics for each site) then stores that information on a file that you can read either as you are online or offline at your leisure. Additionally, these programs will allow you to conduct a search automatically at a designated time. Thus you can enter a search, have the program dial into the Internet overnight, then return to work the next day to find the results of your search clearly organized and summarized in a file. An example of one of these intelligent tools, WebCompass, produced by Quarterdeck corporation (http://www.quarterdeck.com), is shown in Figure 44.

Another search hybrid is called an intelligent agent. These actually work by searching for patterns of information rather than specific words or phrases. Using "fuzzy logic" these agents can actually suggest to a user other ideas that the user has not considered and pursue that information on its own. One unique feature of an agent is that it actually "learns" from its user. Thus as you are conducting a search, you can expand or narrow the information you provide the agent. The agent then uses this new information to increase its accuracy in locating the desired information. An example of the intelligent agent is Autonomy, which is produced by Agentware(http://www.agentware.com). Note that both WebCompass and Autonomy can be downloaded from the manufacturers web site for a 30-day free trial.

Agents and intelligent search engines are rather remarkable resources and undoubtedly as the field of artificial intelligence continues to expand, even more powerful programs will be available to locate and obtain information. However, we would encourage you to try both of the programs we have listed above. By taking the time to use these programs you will be able to more readily locate relevant resources for your students which can then be bookmarked for the students' use. We would also suggest you consider teaching students how to use these programs.

Teacher comments on search engines

Janet, a teacher in California: We find that students spend too much time using a search engine by themselves so we usually have to provide them the addresses of the sites we want them to use. There simply are too many listings when they do a search by themselves so they waste a lot of time trying to find something useful. I know that someday this is something they will need to learn to do by themselves, but right now my objective is to allow them to learn my lesson objectives.

Solomon, a teacher in Maryland: My students will conduct searches in class using a projection device so everyone can see what they are finding. I usually have one group appear before the rest of the class and explain what they are doing and whether the individual results of the search will be useful in the topic we are exploring. This takes quite a bit of time, but I think it helps all the students learn to use search engines.

Jane, a teacher in Colorado: I do the searches by myself using Lycos or AltaVista. When I find sites that will be useful in our lesson, I place them in a folder I create for each class under the "bookmark" menu in my Web browser. When the students get on the Web, they know that the information they need will be found in the sites that appear under the bookmark menu.

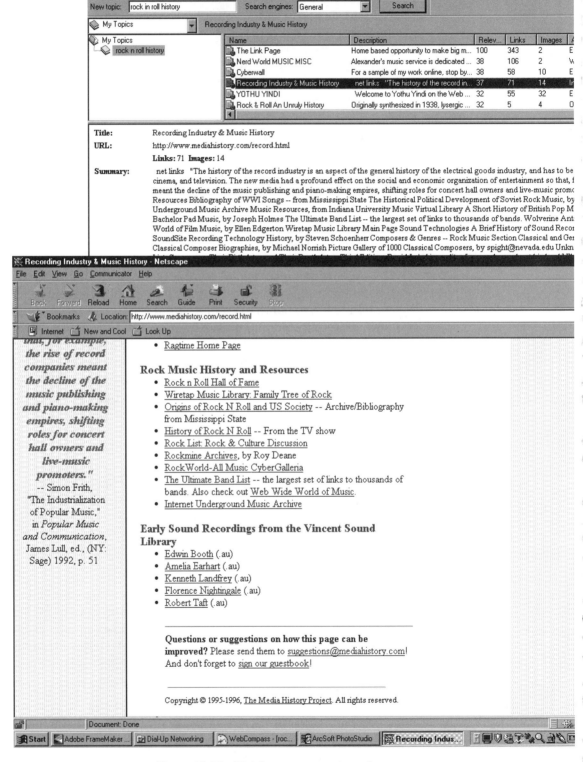

Figure 44: The WebCompass search engine.

Gold mine index for educators

Index sites contain subject or category listings of large numbers of Web sites. Because the sites contain links to Web sites on a given topic, their use can reduce the time required to locate sites through the use of a search engine. Additionally, an index has the advantage of presenting sites that others have found to be particularly useful. As useful as index sites may be, however, they may present two potential problems. First, the sites that are listed often lack a description of their content or potential value to the user. As a result, one may spend a great deal of time roaming from site to site in search of information. Second, index sites can actually contain too many links. One site we recently encountered, for example, was an index containing hundreds of sources of information provided by the U.S. government, grouped under hundreds of distinct topics. Sorting through this particular index would consume an inordinate amount of time—time that could better be devoted to conducting a search on a specific topic of interest.

A good approach to learning to use the Internet is to browse sites of interest. This will give you a good overview of how different sites are organized, how information is presented, and how to navigate within these sites. We suggest you examine the brief descriptions of the "mother lodes" and then connect to these sites so you can evaluate for yourself the diversity of information and resources that are available to educators. This should allow you the opportunity to view content, download files, view a variety of graphics, and to engage in some online searches for information. You will also find these sites to be rich in resources describing the use of the Internet in educational settings. These are good sites in that you will readily gain an appreciation of the educational potential of the Net and the ease of navigating through various sites and menus. It is important to engage in some selective surfing of Internet sites to gain an understanding of its content and the process of navigating the Web.

Internet "mother lodes"

- *Library of Congress* (http://www.loc.gov/)—This site contains a huge global electronic library providing links to libraries around the world. It also contains the Library of Congress online system, information on legislation in the U.S. Congress, copyright information, and a listing of Internet resources.

- *Fedworld* (http://www.fedworld.gov)—Fedworld provides access to more than 100 U.S. government sites and 130 government bulletin boards, including FedWorld Libraries where you can download over 10,000 files. For example, among the many sites under "justice and law," one can locate published decisions of the U.S. Court of Appeals, copyright law information, a search of patent database, and Supreme Court decisions with a search utility to locate decisions.

- CMC's *Applications-Education* (http://www.december.com/cmc/info/applications-education.html)—This site consists of over eighty links to educational resources including the following:

  AskERIC—a federally funded clearinghouse for citations in educational research and lesson plans for applications of technology. A must for educators seeking the latest research and views on educational issues.

  Education—*Yahoo*, an educational element of the Yahoo search engine with links to 68 educational companies, a comprehensive link to sites containing curricular information on literacy, K-12 instruction, math, science, special education, social studies, and foreign languages.

  CISCO—an electronic schoolhouse providing numerous links to libraries, art museums and exhibits, software archives, WWW tools, teaching resources on the Internet, and resources for education planners and administrators.

  Dewey Web—sponsored by Interactive Communications and Simulations and the University of Michigan. This site is an evolving clearinghouse for telecommunications-based education. One component of this site, *Web*ICS provides online telecommunications to link students globally in specific instructional projects.

  Educator's Usenet —a comprehensive list of Usenet newsgroups dedicated to K-12 instruction and educational issues.

  Exploratorium —a collection of over 650 art, science, and human-perception exhibits. Cool graphics!

  K-12 *List*—this site contains links to K-12 school sites that are accessible on the Internet.

  K-12 *Armadillo*—a directory of sites designated as a resource for K-12 classroom instruction. The content of this home page is divided into resources for subject areas (arts, language, geography, history, mathematics, science, social studies, libraries, field trips, museums), educational resources (which includes listings of other K-12 resources), and resources for parents. Teachers will find this a handy source for instructional materials.

  K-12 *Web* 66—THE place to begin the development of a WWW site for your classroom. Designed to aid teachers and students in the design and administration of a school Web site, Web66 also provides valuable information on how a school can set up a LAN, and a WWW, Mail, and ftp server. This site also contains the most comprehensive list of K-12 schools on the Web.

- *Galaxy* (http://galaxy.einet.net/galaxy.html)—A service of EINet, this site contains an extensive set of links to sites addressing law, business and commerce, community, engineering and technology, government, law, leisure and recreation, medicine, reference and interdisciplinary information, science, and social sciences. *Galaxy* also includes a useful search engine to locate specific information/resources.

- *Education Index* (http://www.educationindex.com)—This site contains hundreds of educational links for teachers and parents. Each link listed is accompanied by a descriptive summary of its content. The *Education Index* also contains a discussion group designed to allow teachers the opportunity to exchange ideas and resources on Web related instruction. Sites are listed by subject matter area as well as by age groups.

- AJR *News Link* (http://www.newslink.org/menu.html)—A news page sponsored by the American Journalism Review and Newslink Associates, this site contains links to national and world newspapers, magazines, and radio and TV stations. The site also contains a search engine to allow the user to locate news sources of interest.

CONCLUDING REMARKS

This chapter has presented an overview of ways to communicate and to obtain information on the Internet. In closing, we would like to emphasize three important points related to student access, information sources, and active learning.

First, we would like to address the potential of the Internet to allow all students access to rich educational resources. There is little doubt that the long awaited concept of a global schoolhouse whereby teachers and students can share information, engage in collaborative learning activities, and gain a better appreciation of cultural and linguistic diversity has become a reality. The communication components of the Internet present all students, regardless of geographical location or socioeconomic makeup of the classroom, the opportunity to gain a global perspective on current events and cultural and historical information. Clearly, the extent to which the Internet will be embraced by educators and will fulfill its educational potential remains to be seen. We encourage you, therefore, to carefully consider its potential, to explore the instructional applications of e-mail, discussion groups, and file transfers, and to consider developing your own professional growth program directed at the infusion of communication elements of the Internet into your classroom.

Second, we embrace the notion that the Internet will become the primary source for information used in classroom instruction. As publishers move toward electronic texts that can be customized by the user, and as governmental and institutional agencies place larger amounts of information online, the Internet will be the medium to obtain information that is current, that reflects diverse points of view, and that allows the learner to become more actively involved in constructing meaning. Compared to the traditional classroom textbook, information obtained from the Internet is more current, displays a greater range of perspectives, and, unlike textbooks, it can be modified and updated on a continual basis.

Finally, we acknowledge the potential the communication and informational components of the Internet present in promoting active learning. For example, rather than reading about Russian students in a textbook or periodical, students can engage in direct communication with those students in a meaningful dialog that reflects real-life communication. Moreover, this form of active learning has the advantage of creating an instructional context that is tailored to the objectives of the teacher and the needs of the students themselves. This form of learning should not only be more effective, it should be more relevant for the students, and rewarding to the teacher.

ACTIVITIES

1. E-mail

The following e-mail message was written in Eudora by a ninth grader. The message is being submitted to Supreme Court Justice Sandra Day O'Connor. Examine the message and respond to the following questions:

- Take a look at the "To" line. Why won't this message arrive at Justice O'Connor's office?

- Consider the notion of netiquette. Is this an appropriate tone of language to use if one wants to influence the thinking of a Supreme Court Justice?

- Consider the result of using vague language. Is the author's intent clear?

```
To:        Supreme Court Justice O'Connor@Gov
From:      Justin Smith@lego.k12.com
Subject:   Voting Rights
Cc:
Bcc:
Attachments:

Well, I just thought I'd drop you a quick line to encourage
you to rule favorably on matters that would influence the
ability of teenagers to vote in national elections.

Hope you will consider our constitutional rights too!
```

2. Locating people on the Internet

Connect to Bigfoot (http://www.bigfoot.com), an e-mail search engine. Try searching for

- three of your high school classmates,

- an author of a popular piece of fiction,

- an individual in the business world, and

- a politician in your state.

Once you have located someone, try to see if you can then use the map option from Bigfoot.

3. Discussion groups

Examine the educational discussion groups that appear in this chapter. Subscribe to one that would be of interest to you, and then examine various postings that appear and engage in the following activities:

- Respond to one of the postings using the response or follow-up command on your newsgroup reader.

- Submit your own posting. We would encourage you to inquire as to how others are using the communications elements of the Internet to facilitate classroom instruction.

- Submit an e-mail message to the author of a posting.

4. Locating software on the Internet

- Connect to shareware.com (http://www.shareware.com), a database of over 160,000 software files. Select the "browse" option to examine the various categories and titles of software available for the PC or Macintosh.

- Go to the ZDNet software library (http://www.hotfiles.com/index.html). Examine, then download one of the ten best tool programs.

5. Using search engines

Connect to the All-in-One search page (http://www.albany.net/allinone/all1www.html#WWW). Here you will find links to the following search engines: Yahoo, Lycos, Find-It, Web Index, WebCrawler, InfoSeek, Deja News, EI Net, and Inktomi. Select a topic of interest to you and enter it in several of these search engines. Examine the results of your search by comparing the number of "hits" you receive from each search engine.

CHAPTER 3 — INTERNET RESOURCES: EVALUATING AND INSTRUCTING

OVERVIEW

This chapter is divided into two major sections (Figure 45):

- The first section addresses procedures for students and teachers to assess and evaluate information and other resources found on the Internet.

- The second section presents instructional activities and strategies for using the Internet as a tool to promote learning.

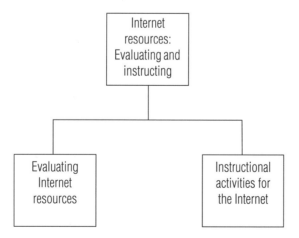

Figure 45: Chapter 3 concept map.

EVALUATING INTERNET RESOURCES

In this section we examine the issue of evaluating information on the Internet. Two general topics will be explored: (1) the need for evaluating information and (2) a practical framework for evaluating information on the Internet.

The need for evaluating information

There is little doubt that the Internet has the potential to provide educators with a tool that can lead to profound changes in the nature of classroom instruction and learning. The immediacy and ease of exploring various sources of information on a global scale will allow students to construct knowledge that is directed by the learner's ability to generate meaningful objectives rather than memorizing the facts and details. This form of learning will require students and teachers to learn how to navigate and acquire information, generate objectives tailored to needs of the classroom, and acquire strategies for sifting through vast amounts of information to generate meaningful and relevant conclusions. The ultimate success of this tool, however, will depend upon students' and teachers' ability not only to examine and make sense of the information they encounter, but also to evaluate the merits of the information itself. In what follows, we will examine the characteristics of information on the Internet, the demands this information places on the learner, and finally we will apply these two factors in establishing a procedure for evaluating information on the Net.

Information on the Internet has three characteristics that distinguish it from traditional classroom materials such as textbooks, supplemental readings, videos, and films. Information on the Internet is *extensive*, *dynamic*, and readily *accessible*. Acknowledging these characteristics will provide a better understanding of the potential as well as the challenges this new instructional tool offers educators.

Information on the Internet is so extensive that the problem isn't finding information; it's determining what to do with the vast amount of information available. Results of a search conducted by Alta Vista or Yahoo, for example, can produce hundreds of sites containing information on a given topic. Because information located at these sites will vary considerably in difficulty, accuracy, quality, and specificity, greater responsibility is placed on the teacher and the student to make decisions about the usefulness of the material examined. And recognizing the paucity of time available for most school learning tasks, making these decisions will have considerable impact on student learning.

A second characteristic of information accessed through the Internet is its dynamic nature. Unlike most traditional forms of classroom materials, information on the Internet exists in a medium that is modified, revised, or deleted with relative ease. As a result, the content at any given site is likely to change in a short period of time as information is added, new links are established between and within sites, or as entire new sites are added to the Net. These changes may occur within minutes, hours, or days. For example, news tickers running on the bottom of your screen can display and update news, weather, sports, and stock market data while you are connected to the Internet. Usenet, listservs, and electronic journals, magazines, and news sources are constantly changing, whereas information sources such as library catalogs and many government sites evolve much more slowly. For classroom instruction that historically has been based on textbooks, transitioning into the dynamic medium of the Internet requires flexibility from both teacher and student. Because classroom instruction can no longer be limited to covering the chapters in the text, teachers will need to focus on sources of information that are both plentiful and also constantly changing. For the teacher, this requires flexibility in the selection of materials and a willingness to modify instruction to meet the demands of an evolving source of information.

A third and final characteristic of information on the Internet is accessibility. By this, we mean that information is obtained immediately, inexpensively, and without a great deal of effort. As students and teachers are provided immediate access to information, strategies will need to be advanced for making decisions as to what information should be used, how the teacher and student selectively use that information, and how to assist the learner in maintaining attention to the flow of information that is related to the task, rather then pursuing another interesting source of information. The extensive, dynamic, and accessible nature of information on the Internet presents new challenges to the learner. Without adequate tools and strategies, students may become overloaded with information, unable to comprehend material written at different levels of complexity, or they may become disoriented in countless links. Before we examine some ways to assist students in dealing with this information, let's examine some of the demands the Internet places on the learner.

Demands that the Internet places on the student

As we have noted, the navigational demands for first-time users are temporary—most students acquire a sound understanding of how to use search engines, establish bookmarks, and download files with relative ease. The demands of dealing with information in a hypertext environment, however, are not addressed with the same level of ease. Later in this chapter we will provide activities and strategies for facilitating students' ability to construct meaning from the Net. Before we examine these strategies, let's first explore the nature of cognition in general and the demands hypertext might place on cognition.

Cognition (often referred to as coming to know) includes such internal processes as learning, perception, comprehension, thinking, memory and attention.[1] Central to cognition is the concept of *schemata*—bundles or packs of information stored in our minds that represent our knowledge about objects, situations, our self, categories, and sequences of action.[2] Schemata provide us processes or procedures for dealing with information.[3] For example, the following paragraph is easy to interpret because it contains information congruent with our existing schemata.

> Ever notice how you react to the telephone that rings while you are in a deep sleep? Often you awake with your heart pounding or perhaps you may awake confused and disoriented. This often occurs because you have entered a deep sleep that shuts out stimuli around you and often places you in a state of dreaming. When the telephone rings, you are brought out of this state abruptly and thus you may feel somewhat disoriented for a few minutes.

This paragraph is easy to understand because we all possess schemata to make this information meaningful and relevant to our personal lives. But when we are overloaded with information or are presented information that we cannot relate to existing schemata, as in the following paragraph, cognition is difficult.

> Covered calls can be written when one sells an option while simultaneously owning the same number of shares on the underlying stock. Writing covered calls, however, can limit the profit potential when there is a strong rise in the underlying stock.

Applying the concept of schemata to the Internet, we can readily appreciate some of the demands placed upon students who encounter new and difficult information. Because there is so much information available, and the nature of this material varies considerably in its complexity, the Internet places unique demands on the learner. These demands are best characterized as

- focusing attention,
- thinking critically, and
- attending to various chunks of information.

Focusing attention relates to the learner's ability to deal with constantly changing streams of information as different links are followed. Because hypertext is composed of such vast linkages of text and visual information, the stream of information itself has no organizing principle. Text becomes nonsequential or nonlinear as branching and links allow the learner choices as to which pathways to follow.[4] The organizing principle becomes, therefore, the learner's interest in seeking the information.[5] And as we have noted, how this information is interpreted will depend on the learner's ability to apply existing schemata.

A second demand of hypertext is thinking critically, or the ability to actively use formal logical procedures to understand the world beyond its literal or surface level meaning.[6] A major element of critical thinking requires learners to obtain and derive meaning from diverse and numerous sources of information and to regulate their own thinking. Hypertext provides this sort of environment for the learner, and in an effort to engage in higher level thinking the learner must attempt to make sense of information synthesized from various links or sites. While all students can successfully engage in critical thinking,[7] most are not proficient in critical thinking tasks.[8] No doubt, if students are to be effective in their ability to draw information from the hypertext environment of the Internet, they will need to acquire specific critical thinking strategies that they can then apply independently. Examples of these will be provided later in this chapter.

A final demand created by the hypertext environment is the ability to deal with different "chunks" of information. Because our cognitive abilities are limited to about five to nine bits of information in a given instance,[9] the massive amounts of information presented on the information highway can place considerable stress on our ability to perceive, discriminate, and comprehend. By chunking information into meaningful categories, groups, or clusters, the amount of information we can deal with can be increased. Note, for example, the following screen display (Figure 46) containing information on lung cancer. In this case, we are actually mislead by the two headings into generating categories that may prove to be inefficient. The first heading, "What is nonsmall cell lung cancer?" leads us to believe that we will encounter information describing the characteristics of nonsmall cell lung cancer. Instead, the paragraph describes the types and incidence of this form of cancer. Similarly, the heading "How is nonsmall cell lung cancer diagnosed?" is useful in chunking information contained in the first sentence of the section; however, the section then goes on to describe how the advancement of cancer is described (regardless of the type of cancer). Now note the effect of chunking information from the reading into the following categories:

*   Ways to diagnose nonsmall cell lung cancer
*   How doctors determine the amount of cancer present

These categories allow one to sort out the relevant information and to provide some structure for the text appearing in the two screens. Although this is a rather simple example of the possible effects of chunking, consider some of the unique elements of hypertext. Hypertext is multilinear—the presentation of information depends on the learner's navigation between and within Web links. As the learner attempts to sift through information obtained from various sites and countless links, it is relatively easy to become overloaded with information. Chunking allows the learner a practical way to impose some sort of structure on the text in order to construct meaning.

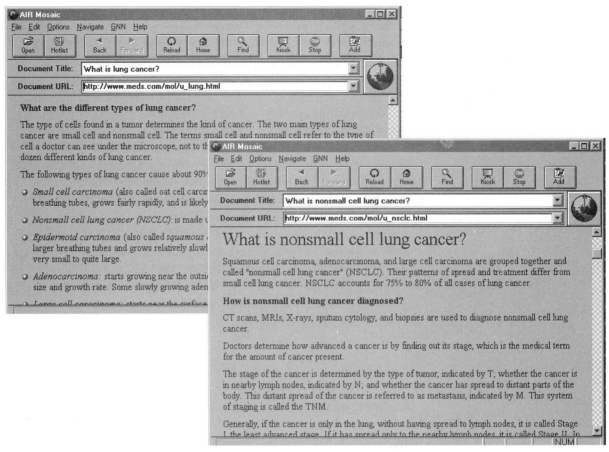

Figure 46: Chunking information.

By now you may recognize that learning in the hypertext environment of the Internet places different demands upon the learner and requires modifications in the nature of classroom instruction. The increased emphasis on focusing one's attention to construct knowledge based on student or teacher generated questions rather than committing the details of a textbook to memory, the need to use critical thinking strategies, and the demands to chunk information into meaningful categories should be acknowledged in planning instruction using the Internet. Similarly, the informational sources the learner accesses must be valid, well organized, and contain an appropriate depth of information. In what follows, we provide some suggestions for evaluating information on the Internet.

A framework for evaluating information

The Internet is a vast resource for exchanging and obtaining information presented in the form of graphics, text, sound, and video. As we have noted, this information is dynamic, accessible, and extensive. However, unlike more traditional forms of educational materials such as textbooks, encyclopedias, and instructional materials published by national professional organizations or educational companies, the content of the Internet is by and large unrestricted. Accordingly, anyone with access to one of the powerful and easy to learn Web authoring programs can create a home page containing content that is a permanent fixture of the Net. Ultimately, then, the recipients of the information must make qualitative judgments as to the merit of the content if they are to construct accurate representations of events or concepts. Unfortunately, many students lack the experience or training to make these judgments, making it necessary for teachers to provide instruction on strategies to evaluate information.

In creating guidelines to evaluate information on the Internet, we have adapted William Katz's criteria for evaluating library reference materials.[10] These criteria, as adapted, include the following:

- Purpose and Audience—What is the intent of this information? Why is it being communicated?

- Authority—What are the credentials of the individual(s) or group(s) presenting this information?

- Scope—What is the breadth, detail of the information provided?

- Format—How is this information presented? Can it be easily interpreted? Can it readily be acquired or reproduced?

- Acceptance of Material—What is the opinion that others have of this material?

To provide a more complete description of these criteria, let's examine how they would apply to information obtained from the Internet.

Purpose: Why is this information being presented?

This is an important criteria, one that should either be obvious to the consumer or stated by the creator of the information. Like the introduction in textbooks, we believe information on the Internet should contain a description of its purpose, its design, and its intended audience. Having this information readily available can save considerable time and minimize frustration. For example, in one of our first efforts to construct a lesson using Internet resources, we decided to focus on the causes and effects of acid rain. Ultimately, it was our goal to present this lesson to middle school teachers in an effort to demonstrate the Internet's instructional applications. Using a search engine, we located a sizeable file containing descriptors that seemingly matched our objectives. So we downloaded the file, printed it, then made copies (the creator of the file encouraged reproductions) and disseminated it to our group. Unfortunately, the teachers soon discovered that our source was actually an effort by the utility industry to rebuke the notion of acid rain altogether and contained little information as to the cause or effects. While embarrassed by our error, we learned a valuable lesson about the importance of acknowledging the creators of the information placed on the Net.

With so much information available on the Internet, we often encounter sources that are in direct contradiction with one another, leaving any conclusions to be drawn by the reader. Here, for example, are two excerpts from Web sites containing information on the impact of chemicals on humans and the content of the book "Our Stolen Future." As you read the two selections, consider the challenges you face in determining the accuracy of the information in each selection and what possible conclusions you might draw regarding the impact of chemicals on human's health.

INTERVIEW: AUTHOR OUTLINES BOOK ON ENDOCRINE DISRUPTERS

Theo Colborn is a senior scientist with the World Wildlife Fund who has spent nearly 10 years studying endocrine-disrupting chemicals. With BOSTON GLOBE reporter Dianne Dumanoski and John Peterson Myers, a zoologist and director of the W. Alton Jones Foundation, Colborn authored the new book "Our Stolen Future," which argues that man-made chemicals may be disrupting the reproductive and intellectual development of humans and wildlife.

GREENWIRE: Could you briefly describe what hormone disrupters are, where they come from, and what they do?

COLBORN: Hormone disrupters are man-made chemicals that have been released into the environment that we now know are capable of penetrating the human body. What we're concerned about in our book is the effect of these chemicals on the unborn, developing embryo, and also what happens to the exposed young individual.

These chemicals come from many sources. Historically, we focused on three particular chemicals-DDT, PCBs and dioxin-because those were the only ones that the scientists had the money to look at.

Recently, through some serendipitous accidents in laboratories, it was also discovered that there are components of plastic products that are biologically active. And even though there are very, very small amounts of these chemicals out there, they are extremely threatening to the developing embryo at very, very small levels. None of these chemicals are lethal or deadly; I hate to see those terms used. And we aren't addressing whether they are carcinogens.

HOW THEY MAY AFFECT YOU

So how do these chemicals affect the embryo? Basically, they inhibit the naturally produced chemicals that control fetal development. They control your body even now: how you think, how you move about, how you metabolize your food, and so on.

(http://www.ecology.com/GREENWRE/archive/311to31596.htm#4)

AGING, CANCER, & HORMONES:OUR FUTURE HAS NOT BEEN STOLEN by Bruce N. Ames

Though some epidemiological studies have found an association between cancer and low levels of industrial pollutants, the results were usually weak, and the studies did not correct for diet, which is potentially, a large confounding factor. There are several toxicological reasons why dietary residues of synthetic chemicals such as pesticides and industrial pollutants are not likely to be significant carcinogenic risks to humans.

1) Animal cancer tests, which are done at the maximum tolerated dose (MTD) of the test chemical, are misinterpreted to mean that low doses of synthetic chemicals and industrial pollutants are relevant to human cancer. Half of all chemicals tested, whether synthetic or natural, are carcinogenic to rodents at the MTD [6]. A plausible explanation for the high proportion of positive results is that testing at the MTD can cause chronic cell killing and consequent cell division due to cell replacement, a risk factor for cancer that can be limited to high doses. Thus it seems likely that a high proportion of all chemicals, whether synthetic or natural, might be "carcinogens" if tested in the standard rodent bioassay at the MTD, but this will be due to the effects of the high doses for non-mutagens, and a synergistic effect of cell division at high doses with DNA damage for the mutagens [6]. Ignoring this greatly exaggerates hypothetical cancer risks calculated for regulatory policy [3-6].

2) The vast bulk of chemicals ingested by humans are natural. For example 99.99% of the pesticides we eat are naturally present in plants to ward off insects and other predators [5]. Half of the natural pesticides tested (33/59) at the MTD are rodent carcinogens [5]. Reducing our exposure to the 0.01% of ingested pesticides that are synthetic is not likely to reduce cancer rates [5]. Synthetic pesticide residues in the U.S. diet rank extremely low compared to the background of natural chemicals when human exposures to rodent carcinogens are ranked according to possible carcinogenic hazard [5].

3) Cooking food generates thousands of chemicals [5]. There are over l000 chemicals reported in a cup of coffee. Only 26 have been tested in animal cancer tests and more than half are rodent carcinogens; there are still a thousand chemicals left to test [5]. The amount of rodent carcinogens consumed as pesticide residues in a year is less than the known amount of rodent carcinogens in a cup of coffee [5]. This does not mean that coffee is dangerous but that animal cancer tests and worst-case risk assessment build in enormous safety factors and should not be considered true risks. Animals and humans can cope with the tremendous variety of natural chemicals because they are extremely well protected by many general-defense enzymes,

93

most of which are inducible (i.e., whenever a defense enzyme is in use, more of it is made) [3]. These defenses are equally effective against natural and synthetic reactive chemicals. One does not expect, nor does one find, a general difference between synthetic and natural chemicals in toxicity or ability to cause cancer in high-dose rodent tests [5]. Thus focussing regulatory attention on tiny traces of synthetic chemicals, while ignoring the enormous natural background, has resulted in an imbalance in the perception of hazard and allocation of resources[7-10].

(http://mendel.berkely.edu/center/ames.capnews.html)

In the case of the Colborn interviews we could assume that there is ample evidence to suggest that chemicals have an effect on human health, while on the other hand the ideas of Bruce Ames would lead us to the conclusion that because so many chemicals are natural, those in synthetic form present far less risk than that presented in Colborn's book.

Authority: What are the qualifications of the person(s) presenting this information?

Publishers of most classroom texts or instructional materials normally adhere to various criteria to ensure that the content is presented by individuals who are knowledgeable in their field. Normally, books are either written by specialists, or specialists serve as consultants to the writing process. Additionally, the cost of producing a text mandates that before it is published, it will undergo rather extensive review by both content experts and practitioners. Thus with some degree of certainty, the user can assume the content to be accurate, up-to-date, and reflect the best thinking on current topics or themes. Producing text or other sorts of information for dissemination on the Net does not necessarily undergo this same process, so it is crucial to gain a sense of the qualifications of the individual(s) who wrote or created the information. Again, let's compare two examples of materials taken from the Internet to determine the role of authority when assessing information.

Smoking depletes the body's supply of Vitamin C, and diets high in sugar need more C to compensate the immune system. Vitamin C strengthens the collagen in the skin, and has just recently been proven to help you live longer!
Neutral C plus is an Ester C (825 mg), which has a neutral pH of 7 that gives it 4 to 5 times greater assimilation and utilization than ascorbic acid, the most common form of Vitamin C. It's natural metabolite complexes carry it directly into the white blood cell. This means that it can enter the bloodstream twice as fast

and is retained nearly three times longer than regular Vitamin C.

> New Vision International, Inc.
> (http://www.halcyon.com/klot/natural/nuhome.html)

> CyberWire Dispatch: The Unabomber
> CyberWire Dispatch // Copyright (c) 1995 // Brock N. Meeks
> Jacking in from the "Where's Pat Garret When You Need Him?" Port:

> Washington, DC -- A stunning transformation is taking place. Thanks to FBI Director Louis Freeh and his merry band of trigger happy goons, the Unabomber is about to make a status leap from Freddie Kruger to folk hero.
> At the behest of the square-jawed "make my day" Freeh, the Washington Post and New York Times today (Tuesday) collaborated -- against their better judgement-- and printed all 35,000 words of the Unabomber's treatise "Industrial Society and its Future."

In the example dealing with vitamin C, the author is unknown. No doubt it was written by individuals responsible for marketing the product, although it presents information that appears to resemble that which may be presented by a nutritionist. In the second example, the author is identified, but we have no information as to his credentials, his affiliation, or his experience in addressing issues of terrorism or criminology.

Scope: What is the breadth of information provided?

Breadth of information refers to the range of content presented on a given topic or theme. Although a textbook's table of contents and index provide a good indication of the breadth of coverage of a topic, information on the Net is more often described in terms of the size of the file (in bytes) or it may be listed by a descriptive title on a Web site containing hundreds of links. As a result, it is often difficult to determine the breadth of coverage given to a given topic or source. For example, the product of a search on jazz history using the Magellan search engine (http://www.mckinley.com/) resulted in the site The Jazz Photography of Ray Avery (http://bookweb.cwis.uci.edu:8042/Jazz/jazz.html) with the following description:

> This is an exhibition of the Jazz Photography of Ray Avery, who has been in the field since 1945. There are links to an entire collection/history of jazz as well as an exhibition bookstore and index of musicians . . . .

When we examined the link to historical information on jazz, we found a one-page description of *Time, Life,* and *Newsweek* articles in 1953-54 that contained articles on jazz, but no information on the history of jazz. And while the discussion was interesting, well written, and rich in its description, it lacked breadth of coverage on the history of jazz. Thus for a student attempting to understand the origins or development of jazz, this source would provide rather limited resources.

At present, the best procedure for assessing the breadth of coverage for a given source is to access the site and examine its contents. Hopefully, as search engines become more powerful and descriptive in their presentation, the task of assessing this factor will become less time-consuming.

Format: How is this information presented? Can it be easily interpreted? Can it readily be acquired or reproduced?

Format is a relatively straightforward criteria based on commonly accepted design for hypertext documents. A poorly designed Web site can be tedious to navigate and likely to produce frustration for the user. Well-designed Web sites will be designed on the basis of the following characteristics:

- Minimal Graphics—Because in-line graphics can take considerable time to download, the size of the graphics should be kept to a minimum. Additionally, when a graphic is presented as a distinct screen (that is, the user has an option to examine the graphic), the size of the file should be indicated so the user can opt not to download large files.

- A Table of Contents—A clearly presented overview should precede the contents, allowing the user to obtain a sense of the breadth or diversity of content covered. Users should be provided options to link directly with each distinct section of the content.

- Citations and Credits—The creator(s) of the information should be acknowledged on the home page. Where a site has established links to other sites, that link should take the user to the home page to acknowledge its creator/author.

- Information on Links—The content of links should be described to avoid unproductive browsing.

- Absence of Dead-end Pages—Pages should always allow the user to return to the home page or to another part of the site.

- Pages Should Present Consistent Options—Each page should contain consistent options and format. For example, links should be presented in the same color and font, graphics used for symbolic notation should be consistent.

- Statements of Reproduction—Each site should indicate its policy for reproducing information contained at that site. Many sites will limit reproduction for educational or noncommercial purposes. Educators should make certain that if a site allows reproduction of its materials for educational purposes that a copy of that statement is placed on file and included in any copies that may be distributed to students, parents, or staff.

Acceptance of Material: What opinion do others have of this material?

One of the best procedures to determine the overall quality and merit of information on the Net is to seek the opinion of colleagues, professional organizations, or agencies. No doubt one of the best indicators of "quality" is the degree to which an instructional resource has been used extensively by your peers. We strongly advocate the use of discussion groups and listservs as a means to obtain information on useful sites and to request the options of others professionals. Not only will this save valuable instructional time, but it will also allow you to obtain additional information on useful Web sites, and it will assist in generating an awareness of the importance of well-designed hypertext documents.

What do teachers have to say about information on the Internet?

From Jane, an 11th grade social studies teacher in Wisconsin: My students are having an incredibly difficult time in attempting to determine the value of material they locate when they engage in a search. They really have no idea as to what is a good source of information. The problem seems to be that they have access to too many sources.

From Evelyn, a middle school teacher in Iowa: I have found that I must provide supervision and guidance when students access information on their own. They don't have the ability to conduct a search in a reasonable amount of time. They tend to spend a great deal of time visiting a site to determine if the material is valuable to them. In the future I will spend more time trying to teach them how to determine if information is useful. They need to learn how to judge the quality of information on the Net.

From Johnny, a 5th grade teacher in Oregon: I personally spend an excessive amount of time trying to determine the worth of information that is on the Net. I find that I must examine material on a site because often it is written by a variety of people. We really need to have some standards of what constitutes valid or well-written material.

From Carol, a high school mathematics teacher: I like my students to use the Net to find sites that contain information that would demonstrate the practical applications of mathematics. I must admit, though, that I would now have to tell my students which sites to visit. The screening of sites became necessary when I found the students devoting a lot of time to browsing and not being able to determine what constitutes quality.

Summing it up: Evaluating information

In this section we have examined factors to consider as you are evaluating information on the Internet. Whereas on the surface it would appear this issue is no different than what we confront when examining and selecting books, visuals, and audio and video tapes in a library, there are some important distinctions. First, as we have noted, the Internet is accessible, dynamic, and extensive. The sheer volume of information, the ease with which it can be placed online, and the ease with which information is changed readily make it distinct from a library or instructional resource center where the flow of materials and information is controlled by key individuals. Students, not teachers, will control the flow and access to information—deciding what materials to access, the usefulness of those materials, and ultimately either drawing upon that material or navigating to other sources. A second distinction between evaluating information on the Internet and that in a library is ownership. Whereas resources in a library are on loan, e-mail, software programs, text files, and graphics can become a permanent possession of the user, essentially allowing the user to construct a personal digital library. With this sense of ownership, it becomes increasingly important for students to learn procedures for selecting information that represents diverse points of view, recognizing bias, misrepresentation, or inaccuracies, and considering the range of quality inherent in the information on the Internet.

INSTRUCTIONAL ACTIVITIES FOR THE INTERNET

In this final section of the chapter, we examine instructional activities and strategies for communicating and for retrieving and filtering information. While we have included examples that apply to specific grade levels or subject matter, our intent is to provide instructional ideas that can be applied across a variety of grade levels and subject matter areas rather than lesson plans designed for a certain grade level or objective. In some instances you may determine it necessary to modify an activity to accommodate the needs of your classroom or the availability of computer hardware.

In what follows we present a number of instructional activities that are applicable to various subject matter areas and grade levels. Most of these activities require relatively little experience using the Internet, and unless otherwise noted, they can be used for individual, small group, or whole class instruction. For convenience we have categorized these activities into two general areas: (1) e-mail and (2) retrieving and filtering information.

E-mail

In Chapter 2 we presented a number of instructional activities with e-mail. Here we will provide some general instructional formats that will be useful in promoting students' ability to engage in meaningful communication and generate knowledge.

Generative writing

E-mail provides a useful medium for collaborative writing/ communication activities between groups of students from various cultural and socioeconomic backgrounds.   Generative writing is a process not unlike a roundtable discussion. Its purpose is to promote problem solving, the formulation of a position, or the presentation of a point of view that is generated by collaborative efforts. These collaborative groups can be established through the use of student-to-student locator groups such as KidLink (http:// www.kidlink.org/) or Intercultural E-mail Classroom Connections (IECC) (http://www.stolaf.edu/network/iecc). The generative writing activity involves the following procedures:

- A problem, question, or task is formulated by the teacher and presented to the students. Students are told that they will generate a written response to the question/problem presented and this response will then be shared with a group of students on the Internet who have been given the same assignment. Students will also be informed that they can anticipate receiving the written product of this effort from other students via e-mail. Students can generate their written response to the question individually or in groups.

- Students and their Internet peers exchange responses via e-mail. (Note that this is a circumstance where an offline mail program, discussed in Chapter 2, is essential.)

- Students are asked to read their peer group's written response and complete the following: (1) note points or information they would like to incorporate in their paper, (2) comment on one aspect of the written response they like best, (3) provide questions to seek clarification or elaboration. Using the e-mail program (Pine, Eudora, Elm), comments and questions are attached to the original e-mail message and returned to the peer group in the form of a "reply." Once this reply is examined, students revise their original written response.

Clearly, this is a rather flexible activity as the length of the writing, the effort placed upon the formulation of the response, and the amount of revision and editing can vary according to the requirements of the teacher, the age and ability of the students, and the level of difficulty of the question or task itself. Regardless of the content of the writing, the activity itself is straightforward, involves little teacher planning, and engages students in an active learning environment. The advantage of conducting the activity through the use of e-mail and the Internet is characterized by the students' ability to obtain the perspective of peers selected from a global community, and interdependency—students must be responsible to their immediate peers as well as their e-mail peers. Here are some examples of applications of this activity.

Integrated lesson involving mathematics and social studies

A group of sixth-graders in Arizona and their peers in Germany are asked to determine the width of two-lane highways, including any paved shoulder, in their respective locations. Students are then asked to determine the total surface area needed for 100 miles of highway where they live. The students in the two locations then exchange their information and are asked to write several paragraphs to explain why there is such a large difference in the total area between the two locations by considering (1) population density, (2) cost of land, and (3) geography of the area.

Lesson involving science

A group of students in the Los Angeles area and in Norway conduct an experiment on ozone levels. The experiment involves stretching rubber bands on a board, then observing the number of days until the bands break. As this is a measure of the amount of ozone in the air, students also maintain daily logs of the temperature, barometric pressure, and wind speed/direction. Students exchange their data and then write a one-page summary as to what conditions may account for the difference in level of ozone. Following the exchange of students' written responses via e-mail and their subsequent revisions based on their peers' feedback, the teachers present a summary of the environmental conditions at each location (amount of pollutants in the air, cars per capita, etc.). Students then consider this information in their final draft of their written response. Note how the teachers' input allows the presentation of information that may have been overlooked by the students.

Lesson involving language arts

Here is a posting we found on the Hilites Mailing List, a service of the Global SchoolNet Foundation (http://gsn.org), by Marsha Browder, a middle school teacher in South Carolina who was seeking e-mail peers to discuss elements of the book *The Sign of the Beaver* by Elizabeth George Speare. Although this activity does not specify a generative writing component, it could readily be modified to adhere to this instructional format.

```
Date: Sept. 20,95 to Oct.30,95
Subject: Lang.Arts & Social Studies
Grade: 4-6
Purpose: Students will share reactions to reading the novel,

        The Sign of the Beaver by E.Speare

Summary: The main characters are two young teens from totally different
cultures who, through no plans of their own, learn from each other skills
that enable them to live in their changing worlds. The story takes place
in the wilderness during the 1700's. It lends itself to great discussions
on issues of survival and relationships between Indians and white
settlers of the American frontier.

Number of Participants: One classroom or group of students.

Discussion Questions:
```

1. What do you admire about Matt? What do you admire about Attean? Why?
2. What would you like to see Matt do differently? Why?
3. What would you like to see Attean do differently? Why?
4. What would you have liked about living during this time period? What wouldn't you have liked? Why?

Project Coordinator: Marsha Browder
EMail address:MBrowder@rsmsbeaufort.sc.Fred.org
        Robert Smalls Middle School
        Rt4 Box210
        Beaufort, SC 29902
        (803) 525-4250

How to Register: We are a 6th grade class who would like to share our reactions & observations through discussion questions with a class or group that has read or is reading The Sign of the Beaver by Speare

Give us- Your full name
        Your Email address
        Your school name
        Your school address
        Your student's answers to the first discussion questions

<mbrowder@beaufort.sc.fred.org>

Cross-cultural perspectives

There is little doubt that e-mail is a powerful tool to allow students from various countries and cultures immediate and direct access to share their views of various social issues, news events, or historical perspectives. These activities may follow various instructional forms. One could engage students in responding to a list of questions on a given topic or event, then comparing and contrasting their responses from various cultural perspectives. Another form may be generative in nature. Here students in various countries or cultures would each respond to unique questions or tasks. For example, middle school aged students from various countries may examine the effect of natural disasters and how their governments respond in an effort to provide assistance to citizens. Students who experienced the recent earthquake in Northridge, California, the hurricane in Hawaii, and the typhoon in Japan would respond to the following questions:

- Describe the extent of damage to physical property such as homes, buildings, and other structures made by people.

- How many people were displaced from their homes?

- What was the extent of injury to people?

- What immediate steps did various forms of government take in response to the disaster?

- In the future, what steps could government take to reduce the effects of this type of disaster?

Responding by e-mail, students share their responses to these questions, then discuss or write a summary as to the effects of various natural disasters, how these disasters are dealt with in different cultures, and to what extent governments could benefit by sharing their approaches to disasters.

Cross-cultural projects on the Internet can involve rather extensive participation over an extended period of time. For example, Roger Willliams, a retired airline pilot, established a project with the Global SchoolNet Foundation (http://gsn.org/) allowing students throughout the world to interact with him as he traveled throughout Russia in his truck. As Roger traveled he provided written updates to project participants via e-mail. Students were encouraged to submit questions to Roger as he traveled, and these questions as well as his responses were posted for all participants to read.

E-mail activities do not have to be as extensive as those we have just described. By limiting objectives and committing to a single communication, activities can be simplified significantly. For example, if students want to determine the dietary habits of their peers throughout the world, a short questionnaire on students' favorite foods and beverages, how often they eat, if they are provided food at school and their reaction to it, and at what times of day they normally eat could be submitted to various locations throughout the world. In the request for assistance, the teacher could note this is a one-time communication. Another example of a limited activity would involve locating groups of students throughout the world, then requesting the students to provide an e-mail response to a set of questions that would highlight cultural variations in their response to Paul Cezanne's impressionist works as they tour Web Museum in Paris (http://www.emf.net/wm/paint/auth/cezanne/).

Clearly, the possibilities of intercultural exchanges and collaboration are endless, limited only by the time and curricular priorities of the teacher or school district. Regardless of the age of the students and the subject matter that may be learned, a few rather simple guidelines will increase the likelihood of a successful cross-cultural experience:

- *Contact project participants well in advance of the beginning of the project.* You are likely to find that your colleagues have numerous questions, comments, and suggestions regarding the instructional activity. Adequate lead time will allow the opportunity for you to have a well-articulated project. Additionally, you are likely to find that teachers everywhere have rather demanding academic schedules. Adequate lead time will allow them to schedule their instruction accordingly.

- *Be sensitive to cultural differences.* Remember that some topics or activities may be excessively controversial or inappropriate in some cultures. Again, it is important to clearly articulate the purpose of the activity and to clearly define your objectives and procedures well in advance. When in doubt about the content, consult your prospective participants.

- *Establish questions/activities in advance and provide that information to prospective participants.* As we have noted elsewhere in this book, e-mail communications across cultural or geographic boundaries can result in misunderstandings. All participants should have a clear sense of the activity's objectives, the involvement and expectations of the students, the duration of the activity, and anticipated outcomes. Failing to address these factors can produce less than satisfying results. Recently, for example, we engaged a group of undergraduate students majoring in education in an activity involving an exploration of the Japanese schools. Three months prior to engaging our students, we solicited assistance from Japanese educators to locate a group of Japanese students who could collaborate in our project and to lay the foundation for the procedures and goals of the activity. Our Japanese counterparts were eager to become involved and meticulous in their efforts in planning a well-designed and meaningful activity. And we were anxious to obtain Japanese students' views toward education. Unfortunately, as our students began exchanging information by e-mail, we soon discovered that we had established ties with a school for American dependents on a U.S. military base in Japan!

- *Establish a timetable and corresponding deadlines with participants.* A clearly defined timetable will reduce the likelihood that your activity is delayed due to participants' failure to meet deadlines. Nothing can be more frustrating than basing your lesson on an e-mail response containing valuable information that is delayed days or weeks. To ensure timely delivery, establish deadlines in advance and clearly articulate those deadlines to students and participating teachers.

To summarize our discussion of the use of e-mail as an instructional activity, we would like to draw your attention to two considerations. First, we would like to reiterate the importance of teaching students appropriate e-mail netiquette. If students are unfamiliar with this form of communication, it is important to take the time to instill in them an appreciation for appropriate behavior. Again, we recommend the use of an Acceptable Use contract signed by parents and students.

A second consideration involves Internet access. Due to the volume of e-mail that may be submitted and received by a single classroom, consider reading and composing messages offline (accomplished by using a mail program such as Eudora or copying a word processing file and inserting it in your online mail program). Offline composition allows students more time to revise and edit their work, particularly when they can use grammar and spelling check features found on most word processing programs. Another advantage of the offline message generation is transportability.

Word processing files readily can be transported between computers, effectively allowing students to compose messages at home, school, or wherever they may access a computer. Finally, as we mentioned in Chapter 2, offline composition increases the availability of Internet access in the classroom, and it is likely to increase time available for revision and editing.

Retrieving and filtering information

In this section we discuss some activities for retrieving and filtering information from Internet sites once those sites have been located using either a search engine or one of the Useful Sites for Educators listed in Chapter 2.

Moving around the large space full of information contained on the Internet can result in the user becoming disoriented and unable to locate the information needed.[11] One solution to this problem is to provide the user guided tours through the hypertext environment by connecting information within a site[12] or by limiting the amount of information examined as one navigates. As students become more familiar with navigational tools, the size of the information space can increase, as can the type of cognitive tasks the students engage in. With this in mind, we will examine two types of information-gathering tasks. The first, and most readily learned task, requires the student to seek a specific piece of data from a given information space. An example of this retrieval task would include locating the number of children under the age of five who were HIV positive in 1990, or the amount of money the U.S. Congress appropriated for AIDS research over the past five years. The second task involves filtering information from an information space. This task requires the student to have a goal or objective in mind, to selectively identify information from a source, then apply that information in constructing a response to a stated objective. For example, with an objective of determining health information efforts to reduce the incidence of those infected with AIDS, a student might examine data over the past ten years to determine the extent of efforts to provide AIDS related health information, what groups of individuals this effort targeted, and data showing the incidence of AIDS and demographic information on those individuals infected with AIDS.

From these examples we note that retrieval of information is relatively easy as it involves searching an information space to locate a single piece of data. Filtering, on the other hand, requires the ability to search the information space, to discriminate as to what pieces of data may be relevant, then to combine that data to generate a response. Retrieval demands the ability to navigate to locate something; filtering requires navigation, sorting the relevant from the irrelevant, combining data, and generating a response requiring the learner to synthesize and apply the data acquired. Following are a variety of activities to engage students in retrieval and filtering information from a single site.

Retrieving information

This is a good starting point for students who are unfamiliar with navigating the hypertext environment of the Web. Due to the difficulty in entering URL addresses, you will find it useful to make use of the bookmark feature of your Web browser.   Adding a bookmark is an easy task. The user simply clicks on the "add a bookmark" (Netscape) or selects the "favorites" category from the menu bar, then clicks on "add to favorites" and the address of the site presently displayed on the screen is automatically saved and will reside on the browser until deleted. Once a bookmark is created the user "clicks" on the name of the Web site appearing in the bookmark list and the browser will automatically connect to the selected site. This avoids errors in entering the URL address or having to recall or retrieve the address itself. Figure 47 is an example of how we set up a bookmark for the National Center for Health Statistics (http://www.cdc.gov) on Netscape Navigator using the bookmark menu.

Although retrieving information from a single Web site may appear to resemble activities commonly used with textbooks, slides, or illustrations in the classroom, the following accommodations will be helpful for engaging your students in activities that involve the Web.

Provide questions or tasks in advance

Knowing what is expected of them will assist students in directing their attention to the appropriate information, thus reducing the time for online examination of the material. Additionally, taking a few moments to discuss the questions or tasks prior to retrieving information provides students an opportunity to ask questions and clarify your objectives. For example, if students will navigate through a number of Web sites dealing with whales, it would be important to provide students a clearly defined goal as they navigate through the sites as well as how they will apply that information to your instructional goal. We have found it useful to provide students with a handout that provides them their task, but also provides a roadmap of where to travel on the Web, and what to look for at each site. It is important to provide them with a purpose.

Consider collaborative information retrieval

Providing distinct questions to groups of students will minimize online time, promote student interdependence, and provide the teacher the opportunity to gain immediate feedback on students' ability to retrieve information. For example, using the information in Figures 48 and 49, the teacher may provide the following sets of questions to collaborative groups, then ask them to examine the selection to retrieve the desired information.

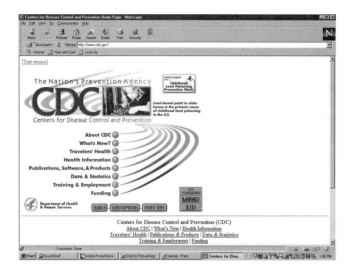

First, go to the WWW page
you want bookmarked.

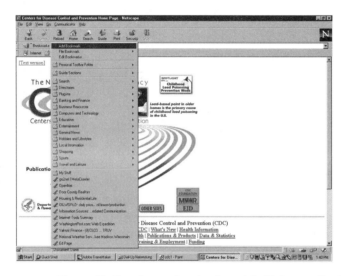

Then add the page's
location to the
bookmark list.

Figure 47: How to create a bookmark in Netscape Navigator.

Set One

1. How many people visited hospital emergency departments for injuries in 1992?

2. How many total visits were there to emergency room departments for all types of medical problems in 1992?

3. Why are more young adults (age 15-24) making more injury visits to emergency rooms than other age groups?

Set Two

1. How many total visits were made to emergency rooms, doctor's offices, and outpatient departments for injuries in 1992?

2. If the population of the U.S. in 1992 was about 250 million, what

percent of the population visited an emergency room?

Set Three

1. What was the average cost for an emergency room visit in 1992? (Note: First find the total number of injury-related visits, then the total costs of these visits. Then divide cost by total number.)

Once the student groups have generated a response to their respective set of questions, the teacher presents a focus question designed to have students synthesize information produced from the responses to all of the questions. For example, students may be asked to consider if health care costs could be significantly reduced by reducing the use of emergency departments and if so, what steps could be taken to reduce their use. Following the presentation of this question, the answers to the collaborative questions are shared and discussed by the class and information obtained from the answers applied to the focus question. This strategy allows students to begin to recognize the process of synthesizing information—a task frequently encountered on the Internet.

Have students reflect on and describe the steps they take to retrieve information

Navigating through a hypertext environment to retrieve information places unique demands on the learner. Learning how to navigate around a given site, using links to move from one screen to another, and adjusting to the diverse styles and formats of each site requires the acquisition of new approaches to dealing with information. Students become more aware of their own cognitive strategies when provided an opportunity to discuss their processing of hypertext openly in class. Hopefully, as students gain insight into the strategies used by their peers, they will gain a more thorough understanding of their own thinking.

Retrieving information from a single Web site is a straightforward task, often resembling activities centered around a text selection or visual image. One distinction, however, is the element of access. Students normally have immediate access to classroom text material. Information retrieved from the Internet, however, is less accessible. If students recognize an error or desire additional information to respond to a question or learning task, it may be difficult to gain additional Internet access time. We reiterate, therefore, the importance of providing clear objectives for learning, discussing with students their personal strategies for navigating and retrieving information when they are online, and promoting activities that allow students the opportunity to apply information to a rich and authentic learning task.

Cautionary note on retrieving information

No doubt by now you realize the ease of locating and

National Center for Health Statistics (NCHS)
Monitoring Health Care in America
Quarterly Fact Sheet
September 1995
SPOTLIGHT ON: INJURIES

There were approximately 34 million injury-related visits to hospital emergency departments (ED) in 1992, or 40 percent of all ED visits. Males had a significantly higher rate of injury visits than females, and youths aged 15-24 years had the highest rate of any age group. Over 9.2 billion dollars were spent on injury-related (ED) visits in 1992.

ACCIDENTAL FALLS MOST COMMON
Accidental falls account for 23 percent of all injury-related ED visits, followed by motor vehicle accidents (12 percent); accidentally being struck by people, objects, or falling objects (11 percent); cuts or punctures by sharp objects (9 percent); and violence (5 percent). In 1993 there were over 145,000 deaths attributed to injury-related causes such as accidents and adverse effects, suicide, and homicide and legal intervention. Accidents were the fifth leading cause of death in 1993, while suicide was the ninth leading cause and homicide was the tenth leading cause.

DOCTOR VISITS
There were 23.8 million office visits to physicians because of injuries in 1992, accounting for 3 percent of all patient visits. Injuries and poisoning were responsible for 7.5 percent of all principal diagnoses for patients in 1992, a total of 57.4 million diagnoses. Sprains and strains of the back alone accounted for more than 7.7 million principal diagnoses in 1992.

OUTPATIENT, INPATIENT VISITS
Over 2.4 million visits to hospital outpatient departments in 1992 were due to injuries, accounting for over 4 percent of all outpatient visits. Back symptoms were responsible for 763,000 or 1.3 percent of all visits, while knee symptoms accounted for 535,000 visits or 1 percent of the total. Back disorders were the principal diagnosis for 679,000 outpatient visits.

In 1993 there were over 2.7 million patients discharged from short-stay hospitals due to injuries. Over one million of these patients were discharged for fractures, 160,000 were discharged for intracranial injuries, and 171,000 were discharged for lacerations and open wounds. Patients admitted for injury and poisoning stayed an average of 6.4 days in the hospital (7.5 days for fractures, 7.3 days for intracranial injuries, and 3.7 days for lacerations and open wounds).

HEALTH INSURANCE COVERAGE
Over 17 percent of the under 65 years of age population -- or 40 million Americans -- had no health insurance coverage in 1993. Nearly 8.4 million children under 15 years of age were uninsured. One out of three Hispanic Americans, one out of four Black Americans, and one out of six White Americans under 65 years of age had no insurance. Among Hispanics, nearly 40 percent of Mexican Americans, 21 percent of Puerto Ricans, and 17 percent of Cubans were uninsured in 1993.

Figure 48: (Part 1) Sample information for collaborative questioning.

Over 42 million Americans, or 16 percent of the population, were enrolled in health maintenance organizations (HMOs) in 1994, twice as many as in 1985 and 7 times as many as in 1976. Thirty-eight percent of enrollees belonged to individual practice associations, while 32 percent belonged to group associations and another 30 percent belonged to mixed plans.

Meanwhile, between 1991 and 1994, private employers' health insurance costs per employee-hour worked increased by 24 percent, to $1.14 an hour. In comparison, wages and salaries per employee-hour worked increased by 9 percent during the same period.

HEALTH EXPENDITURES

Personal health expenditures in the U.S. totaled over $782 billion in 1993, more than triple the total in 1980. Hospital care expenditures accounted for $327 billion or 42 percent of the total, while physician services cost $171 billion (22 percent) and nursing home care costs totaled 69.9 billion or 9 percent of the total.

For more information or to arrange an interview with the author, please contact NCHS, Office of Public Affairs (301) 436-7551, or via e-mail at paoquery@nch10.em.cdc.gov.

Figure 49: (Part 2) Sample information for collaborative questioning.

reproducing information on the WWW. Once information is located, it can be downloaded to disk, printed from the screen, or one can highlight information with the mouse and "copy and paste" it into a word processing program.

This certainly expedites the process of customizing text, but it also presents an environment that invites students to plagiarize and ignore intellectual property rights. Unfortunately, this is quickly becoming a major concern as more students gain access to the Internet. We urge you to use the information provided by the Electronic Frontier Foundation's Web site (http://www.eff.org/pub/Intellectual_property/). Here you will find articles on legal issues relating to cyberspace and links to a multitude of sites dedicated to copyright and intellectual property rights.

Addressing this problem will require a process for educating students, teachers, and parents on the use of copyrighted material and intellectual property rights. Additionally, we would encourage educators to include copyright restrictions and plagiarizing from electronic text as topics in their Acceptable Use Policy. Oh, and one more consideration: There are numerous commercial ventures on the Net that provide students ready access to term papers and theses. This is increasingly becoming a problem as students acquire knowledge of the resources of the Net and as commercial sites believe they can market these papers. Take a few moments to conduct a search using the phrase "term papers" and examine some of these sites.

FILTERING INFORMATION

This requires students to have an objective in mind, to examine various information, to select information relevant to the objective, to discard or gloss over information not relevant to the objective, to synthesize information that assists in accomplishing the objective, then reacting or responding to the objective. Unlike retrieval of information, filtering requires selective attention to various forms of information that are collectively applied to tasks involving higher-level thinking, problem solving, drawing conclusions, or generating hypotheses. Activities of this nature require the teacher or student to first generate a higher-level thinking task, then explore, examine, and retrieve information on the Web that will assist in accomplishing the learning task.

Strategies to assist students in filtering information

Because of the difficulty in keeping track of information within and between Web sites and the lack of structure inherent in the hypertext environment,[13] students can benefit from organizational strategies that link attributes of what they know to the content of the hypertext site.[14] These strategies are effective both in activating students' schemata related to the information encountered and in modifying existing schemata.[15] One group of organizational strategies, graphic organizers, provides the learner pictorial representations of the relationships between facts and concepts, allowing a framework for organizing information and focusing the learner's attention. In what follows we present two types of graphic organizers: concept maps and frames.

Concept Maps

Concept maps are graphic displays of concepts and information and the relationships between them. Generally, the content of the map proceeds from the general to the specific. (Figure 50 is an example of a concept map.) Concept maps contain several distinctive elements. First, conceptual linkages and relationships are displayed by the use of shapes and lines. These visual symbols readily draw students' attention, directing it to important concepts. Second, the concept map contains a variety of graphical forms to draw attention to hierarchical relationships. Note in Figure 50 the use of a rectangle for the title, ovals for the four major concepts, and the absence of graphical forms around the details appearing below the four concepts. Finally, the concept map presents a visual and conceptual organization that is well organized, descriptive, and relevant to the teacher's objectives. Again, turning to Figure 50, the visual arrangement is organized in a hierarchical manner (proceeds from general to specific) and can be interpreted without explanation. Also note that a concept map, unlike an outline, is not

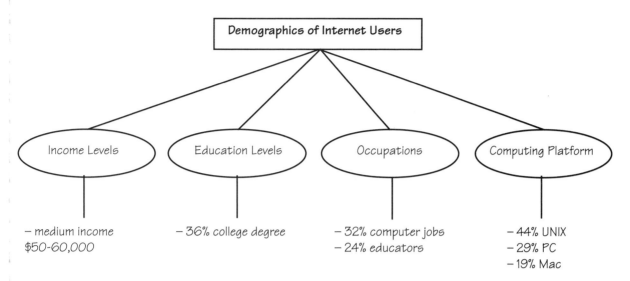

Figure 50: Concept map.

an attempt to "map" the entire content of a reading. Rather, it reflects information the teacher or student determines relevant to the stated objective or content of the lesson.

Figure 51 is an example of a concept map designed to assist students in filtering information on the Internet. What appears here

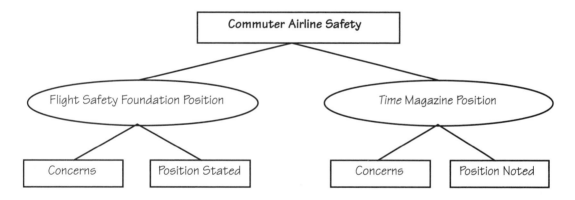

Figure 51: Concept map designed to assist students filter information.

is a concept map addressing the safety of commuter airlines. In this case, students examined a document by the Flight Safety Foundation (http://web.fie.com/web/fed/faa/text/faatsf25.htm) (Figure 52) and an article in *Time* magazine (http://www.pathfinder.com) (Figure 53) focusing on recent commuter airline accidents. Examine this map carefully, then read the selection by Stewart Matthews to locate information related to the left side of the map and the portions of a *Time* magazine article by John Farley to complete the right side of the map.

In completing the concept map, you may have become aware

FSF's Matthews Says Recent Reports Misrepresent Commercial Aviation
Safety Record, Needlessly Alarm Public
Release Date: December 9, 1994
Contact: Girard Steichen, assistant director of publications
Commercial air travel is indisputably the safest form of mass transportation available today, despite recent reports that question the industry's overall safety record, Flight Safety Foundation (FSF) President, Chairman and CEO Stuart Matthews says.

"The flying public is being misled and needlessly alarmed by flawed press reports on aviation accidents and incidents, and hysterical accounts of the industry's performance," Matthews said.

Matthews, responding to some recent press reports and industry statements about aviation safety following recent fatal U.S. airline and commuter accidents, added: "No other industry has as much invested and as much at stake in safety as the aviation industry. Industry standards and performance are outstanding, which a close look at the record proves."

Recent U.S. fatal aircraft accidents, including a USAir Boeing 737 crash near Pittsburgh, Pennsylvania, and the crash of an American Eagle ATR-72 commuter in Indiana, have brought intense media scrutiny on commercial air transport operations, government regulations and the industry's safety record. Much of that attention has centered on commuter operations that operate under less stringent federal regulations than large airlines, although safety questions have been raised about the industry as a whole, Matthews said.

The commuter industry's safety record has been skewed by the method used to categorize accident statistics, Matthews said. The commuter category has included hazardous operations such as "bush" flying in Alaska. Moreover, FAA statistics indicated that 15 percent of all commuter accidents involve training flights with no passengers.

The most recent full-year statistics compiled by the U.S. Federal Aviation Administration (FAA) indicated that in 1993 the commuter accident rate (excluding Alaskan operations and helicopter operations) was 3.7 accidents per 100,000 departures, compared with 2.9 accidents per 100,000 departures for larger airlines (operating aircraft with more than 30 seats). While emphasizing that the accident rates were similar, Matthews noted that a single accident can distort such low statistics.

Figure 52: Flight Safety Foundation document for concept map filter.

that the map's organizational structure directed your attention as you read the text selections. By screening irrelevant information and attending to information related to the conceptual categories of "concerns" and "positions," you were able to focus your attention and filter information.

Here are the steps in constructing a concept map for use with Internet materials:

Step One: Determine the relevant concepts contained in the material

Prior to having students examine information on the Internet, peruse that material in an effort to note concepts (a label used to describe objects or events that share certain characteristics) and words or phrases that describe how information can be associated with the selected concepts. Note that a concept map is not an outline because it is limited to concepts and information that are relevant to your objectives or objectives of the students. An outline, on the other hand, is an effort to structure all conceptual elements regardless of their importance. Our experience with concept maps suggests that it is sometimes difficult to identify concepts when dealing with poorly written text or poorly presented information. In this circumstance you will find it useful to draw upon your own knowledge to present concepts that may be lacking in the text information.

Step Two: Organize concepts and identify linkages

Construction of the map begins with a title that is brief and descriptive of the content. Elements of the map are then identified by first listing major concepts, then determining if these concepts are superordinate or coordinate to one another. Finally, information associated with the concepts is identified and placed under the appropriate conceptual label.

Step Three: Refine and elaborate

The final step involves attention to inserting markers that demonstrate conceptual and locational linkages. Conceptual linkages are established by using certain shapes for different levels of conceptualization and lines to draw the learners' attention to supporting information. Locational linkages are marked by placing URL addresses or bookmark titles in the material adjacent to the corresponding labels or information in the map.

Constructing a concept map

Here is an example of the three-step process of constructing a concept map to accompany a unit on global warming, where the objective is to have students explore some of the possible effects of global warming on humans:

1. A search engine is used to locate sources of information on global warming. Using the descriptions of the sites retrieved from the search, those that appear to contain information related to the selected topic are quickly scanned for their

TIME

December 26, 1994 Volume 144, No. 26
AIR SAFETY UNDER A CLOUD
By CHRISTOPHER JOHN FARLEY

Airline safety is coming under increased scrutiny in the midst of the holiday travel season, the most awkward time for a crisis of confidence in air travel. A recent string of airline crashes and mishaps has compelled passengers, federal regulators and aviation experts to take a suddenly more skeptical look at an industry that had steadily been improving its safety record over the years. Statistically, air travel remains more than 100 times as safe as travel by car. But so far this year, more than 250 people have been killed in air crashes within the U.S.

A conspicuous number of crashes have involved commuter airlines, including the October wreck of an American Eagle ATR-72 in Indiana that killed all 68 people on board. One reason for the increased number of commuter crashes is simply growth in traffic. Regional airlines that tend to operate smaller, prop-driven planes carried 50 million passengers in 1993, up from 15 million in 1980.

After the crash of the American Eagle ATR-72, the Federal Aviation Administration barred ATR model planes from flying in icy weather. That forced the carrier to move other planes more suitable to cold conditions to northern cities. But late last week, American Eagle canceled all its flights at Chicago's busy O'Hare International Airport after a pilots' union complained that the replacement fleet's crews had not adequately been trained to fly during cold weather.

In one of the most severe setbacks for the commuter-airline industry, the International Airline Passengers Association warned members about flying in planes with 30 seats or fewer. Some airline experts said the association, which also sells insurance to passengers, was overreacting. Says Aaron Gellman, director of the Transportation Center at Northwestern University: "It's not against their financial interests to make people worried."

But government officials were also becoming increasingly concerned. Last week, after touring the muddy crash site of Flight 3379, Transportation Secretary Federico Pena said that within 100 days, tougher safety regulations for small commuter planes will be formulated. He also announced plans to bring aircraft makers, pilots and other industry members to Washington for an aviation-safety summit. Jerome Lederer, president emeritus of the Flight Safety Foundation, says the airline industry needs to take advice from people in the field: "The airlines express an interest in safety, but the guys in the shops regularly are not consulted." Other experts say the problem lies not in the plane hangars but in the offices of the FAA. An aviation authority says the agency should have grounded the foreign-made ATRs long ago, but "the U.S. government didn't want to offend foreign countries like France."

Figure 53: Time magazine article for concept map filter.

general content. When a site appears to be suitable, the general concepts or topics addressed in the information that are related to the stated lesson objective are listed. Here, for example, are relevant topics contained in the World Health Organization's information on the health effects of global warming (http://www.ciesn.org/docs/001-007/001/007.html): Thermal Factors, Heat Disorders, Ultraviolet Radiation, Skin Cancers, Eye Diseases, Air Pollution. And here are topics acquired from a site (http://ciesin.org/docs/001-338/001-338.html) displaying a paper produced by the Environmental Protection Agency addressing the possible health effects of global weather changes brought about by global warming:[16] Increased Snowfall, Low Humidity in Winter, Rapid Weather Changes, Increase in Temperature Extremes.

2. Next, all topics identified from the two sites are examined, a title is generated, and the topics are arranged to display superordinate/subordinate/coordinate relationships (Table 12).

Human Health	Weather Changes
Thermal Factors	Increased Snowfall
Heat Disorders	Low Humidity in Winter
Ultraviolet Radiation	Rapid Weather Changes
Skin Cancers	Increase in Temperature Extremes
Eye Diseases	
Air Pollution	

Table 12: Potential effects of global warming.

3. Finally, the concept map (Figure 54) is refined by inserting appropriate conceptual markers and associations.

There are several noteworthy features of the concept map in Figure 54. First, we have inserted the bookmark titles below the respective labels to direct the student to the appropriate Web site. Second, economic and health implications have been added at the bottom of the map to allow the student to generate information based on the content of the Web site. Note also that spaces have been provided for the insertion of additional information under the labels health problems, environmental risks, and seasonal effects. And, finally, at the bottom of the map the student is asked to apply information obtained from the concepts highlighted in the map and corresponding portions of the Web site to reach some form of conclusion as to the significance of efforts to reduce global warming.

Concept maps provide a powerful strategy to assist students in locating, selecting, integrating, and restructuring information on the Net. Their use provides a conceptual structure that can activate students' prior knowledge, direct their attention to relevant

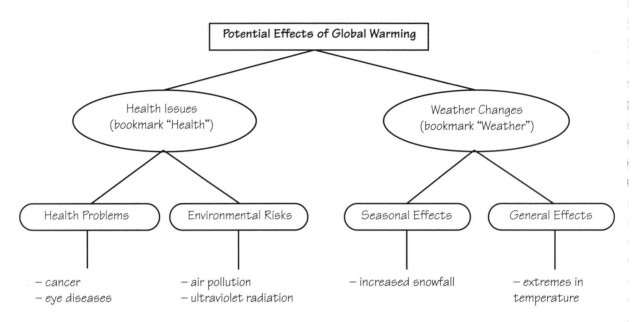

Figure 54: Conclusions regarding the importance of programs attempting to reduce global warming.

information they encounter at Net sites, and thereby provide an informational or conceptual base from which students can engage in higher-level thinking.

Frames

A second strategy to assist students to filter information is using a frame. Frames are pictorial representations of information in the form of a grid or matrix. Their function is to present a pictorial display of the conceptual organization of information in the form of a two-dimensional matrix where concepts are presented in rows and columns, and information is presented in the boxes, or slots, as shown in Table 13.

	Angles	Sides	Area
Rectangle	all right	all parallel	L x W
Parallelogram	opposite equal	2 parallel	L x W
Square	all right	all equal all parallel	L x W

Table 13: Frame for types of trapezoids.

In this frame the slots, or boxes, contain information regarding the characteristics (the labels in the columns) for the three types of trapezoids (the labels for the rows). Thus, the respective slots for the square indicate its angles are right angles, all sides are parallel, and its area is calculated by multiplying its length by its width.

Constructing frames that will assist students in filtering information located on the Net is accomplished by the following three steps:

1. Once the teacher has selected some global objectives for a unit of study, Net sites are located through appropriate search engines. Once these sites have been selected, the teacher identifies the major ideas, concepts, and principles in the material that will assist in the lesson objective.

2. Following an examination of the information contained on the Internet, the teacher can determine which type of frame can best facilitate the organization of the information. Three types of frames can be used. The matrix, or attribute, frame addresses certain characteristics of a group of concepts or objects (see Table 14). A goal frame highlights the goal of an event or problem, the plan defined to meet the goal, the result of the plan, and the final outcome of the event or problem (see Table 15). Finally, the problem-solution frame identifies a given problem, action that is taken to address the issue, and the resolution or consequence of the action (see Table 16).

	Executive	**Judicial**	**Legislative**
How position obtained	elected	appointed	elected
Length of term	4 years	life	2 or 4 years
Daily functions directed by	party politics	Constitution	party politics

Table 14: Attribute frame of federal government.

	Goal	**Plan**	**Result**	**Long-term outcomes**
Reduction of consumption of fossil fuels	Reduce oil consumption by lowering gas consumption	Increase fuel efficiency of automobile, lower speed limit, increase energy efficiency	Reduced per capita consumption of oil	Increase standard of living
Disposal of low-level radioactive wastes	Provide safe disposal of low-level radioactive materials	Construct national repository	Inability to locate safe structure	Waste piling up at nuclear sites

Table 15: Goal frame for environmental efforts.

	Problem	**Action**	**Results**
Federal government legislative efforts	High costs of medical insurance, many uninsured citizens	Introduction of health care proposal	No legislative action
Private sector efforts	High costs of insurance, possible government regulation	Restructuring to reduce costs	Rate of health care cost increases declines

Table 16: Problem-solution frame of government and private sector efforts to reduce health care costs.

3. Provide students with a partially completed frame where columns and rows have been labeled and slots remain empty. Indicate the source of information to be used (the URL address or bookmark title), then direct students to locate information from the Net sources that will assist them in completing the frame.

Table 17 is a frame constructed for a group of ninth-graders studying the effects of smoking and people's views on smoking. The information appearing in the slots, obtained from the RJ Reynolds Smokers Rights Action Guide (http://www.cris.com/ ~trieger/rights.shtml) and the Canadian Council on Smoking and Health (http://fox.nstn.ca/~ncth2/ncdo.html) was generated by the students.

	Position on smoking	**Goal/action of group**	**Health effects of smoking**
Smokers rights groups	• believe that smoking bans hurt business • not letting people smoke reduces taxes that are collected in bars and cafes	• goal is to change laws or stop laws from interfering with smokers • action is to contact politicians and speak at meetings	• this group does not acknowledge any health effects of smoking
Nonsmoking groups	• believe that smoking carries many health risks that are additive	• quit smoking	• 20% of deaths in Canada caused by smoking • reduces lifespan by 15 years • causes asthma, strokes, heart disease, and cancer

Table 17: Positions of nonsmoking and smoking rights groups.

The frame's flexibility allows it to be used for numerous instructional applications. In a cooperative learning setting, groups can be assigned the task of obtaining information for a particular slot, thus minimizing the amount of time required to locate and filter information. Having located information, the frame is completed as a class activity as each group presents their respective information. As a means to promote writing, the frame can serve as the organizational tool for the writer, with the rows or columns serving as the content for the topic sentence or hypothesis, and information in the slots serving as supporting information. The act of writing from a frame allows students to reflect upon the content, to elaborate or better recognize relationships among concepts or ideas, and to note distinctions between information. And as a strategy to assist students in generating their own questions or problems, the frame can act as a tool for planning the topics or concepts to explore, the characteristics of those concepts that might be examined, and to consider relationships between various concepts examined. Once the structure of the frame is defined, students can explore the Internet for the appropriate information either through conducting a search or by being directed to specific sites by the teacher.

Concluding remarks on strategies to assist students filter information

As a classroom learning tool, the Internet provides information that possesses a level of depth and breadth that is unprecedented in classroom learning. With so much information to chose from, teachers and students can readily suffer from an overload of information, can become lost in a plethora of links between Web sites, or they can lose sight of their objectives as their attention is directed to interesting or unusual information. Traditionally, textbooks have served as the instructional lighthouse. Teachers are drawn to the content which by nature defines learning objectives. Students are drawn to the content because its there. Thus they carefully read the text's content, commit the content to memory, and practice some sort of retrieval or recall process for the purpose of completing various forms of assessment devices administered by the teacher. As a source of information, the Internet is too unwieldy to serve as a lighthouse—it contains too much information, and because of numerous links between sites, the information doesn't present itself in a linear fashion. For this reason, the use of strategies such as concept maps, frames, or other strategies that organize information and direct the student's attention are essential in advancing the notion of generative learning—learning characterized by the formulation of a problem or question, then seeking information to solve the problem in an environment of collaborative learning, active involvement, and authentic learning tasks.

There are numerous sites on the Internet that provide interesting information and instructional activities for students. Some, such as NASA's Quest program (http://quest.arc.nasa.gov), provide stimulating lessons that include e-mail resources, text files, archives of pictures associated with the specific lesson, bibliographies, links to sites with supporting information, teacher's guide and classroom activities, field journals, and a fascinating question-answer archive containing questions and answers submitted by various scientists involved in the projects. Due to the evolving nature of educational materials on the Internet, we have chosen to place a rather comprehensive annotated list of these sites, including links, on this text's home page. This will allow us to provide you with a more recent resource for instructional activities on the Internet, an opportunity to post your responses to various activities contained on the Internet or listed in this book, and to provide a forum for discussion of issues pertaining to the use of the Internet in the classroom.

CONCLUDING REMARKS

This chapter has presented ways to evaluate Internet resources and general activities and strategies that can be used in assisting students' learning. As we conclude our discussion of these topics, we call your attention to three points related to assessing resources and creating instruction that is centered on the use of the Internet. First, we emphasize the importance of considering the nature of the resources that you select for your students as well as those accessed by students as they explore the Net. Unlike materials that are located in a library, a school district media collection, or those marketed by publishers, there is no assumed level of quality assurance of material on the Net. Accordingly, using good judgment, considering the factors we have highlighted in this chapter, and taking the time to teach your students to adopt some form of quality control standards will help alleviate the problem of using resources that are inaccurate, inane, or highly subjective in their presentation. Whereas the majority of material we have encountered is accurate, remember that, at present, the Internet is a relatively unregulated medium.

Second, we have taken great care in limiting our presentation of activities to those that are supported by research and accepted educational practice. As with any novel instructional technology, it is relatively easy to generate a cookbook of activities that may appear to be interesting, motivating for students, and that can immediately be incorporated into classroom instruction. Unfortunately, although we have encountered numerous suggestions for instructional activities centered around the use of the Internet in discussion groups, mailing lists, and in journals and newsletters, we are hesitant to embrace these suggestions wholeheartedly. In some instances these instructional activities are likely to be motivating to students, but possess little educational merit. In other instances the activities are likely to be interesting and display some sound applications of the Internet, but are not likely to be tailored to teacher or student objectives. Given these concerns and the limited Internet access time individual students are likely to have available in the school setting, we encourage educators to focus their efforts on instructional activities that address relevant objectives, are tailored to the needs of the students, and that will assist students in acquiring strategies they can apply to a variety of authentic learning tasks.

A third and final point is to reiterate the observation regarding the difficulty students are likely to face in sorting out information as they navigate through a series of sites through various links. The ability to access a multitude of sources rapidly is a powerful feature of the Internet. Yet, that same feature presents students a learning environment far removed from more conventional sources of information such as textbooks. Successful application of the hypertext environment is likely to require appropriate training on its use for teacher and student. You may consider, therefore, the advantages of learning this new medium as a collaborative effort between teacher and student. In particular, take time to carefully describe the procedures for a given lesson, ask students to discuss problems as they are encountered, and as a class reflect on your application of the Internet when you complete an activity or assignment. Engaging in reflective thought on how you used the Net, on strategies that assisted in meeting objectives, and on problems in its application that remain unresolved are useful issues to stimulate a meaningful dialog with your students.

ACTIVITIES

1. Instructional activities

There are numerous instructional activities presented on mailing lists, Web sites, and in newsgroups. It is important to distinguish between those resources that provide activities that promote the use of the Internet for learning and those that use the Internet as a means to disseminate lesson plans structured around resources offline. Here, for example, is a lesson plan that appeared in ASK ERIC. Examine this activity, then determine how you might modify it to allow students to draw upon various Internet resources in responding to the questions and activities listed.

The Changing Role of the Iron Range
Submitted by: Stacey M. Loerts
Endorsed by: Don Descy
Mankato State University
Grade Level: Grades 4-5
Description:

The iron range located in northern Minnesota is a unique geographical area that can teach children many valuable things. It can teach students about maps, immigration, and natural resources. This lesson teaches students about mining, natural resources, and economies. The iron range is used as a case study. We will be tracking ore mining to taconite to tourism. Children will learn the changing economic function of the iron range.

Goal:

Students will have an understanding of the role that natural resources has on economies.

Objectives:

1. The students will list three different eras the iron range

has gone through since the late 1800s.

2. The students will define what economy means.

3. Students will list at least three reasons why the iron range's economy has changed since the late 1800s.

4. The students tell of the destruction to the land that mining causes.

Background information:

The iron range is located in the northern part of Minnesota. It is comprised of many little towns that were once thriving; many are now becoming ghost towns. The area was developed in the late 1800s and many emigrants came to the area to work in the mines. The iron ore has been depleted since then and the land is barren.

Today many people are hoping that development of taconite will revive the area. Tourism is also playing a part in the revival of the economies in the little towns around the iron range.

Concepts:

Students will be able to:

1. Relate natural resources to the economy and what causes areas to prosper or become stagnated.

2. Apply these concepts to their own city or town.

3. Identify the importance of natural resources and realize that they do run out.

Materials:

Piece of real ore and taconite. Articles about taconite and ore. Pictures of the iron range. Text that discusses economies.

Procedure:

1. Hang pictures of the iron range up and around the room, display a bulletin board, set pieces of real ore and taconite out. Let the children explore these things on their own. This will hopefully raise questions.

2. Handout articles about ore. Read as a class.

3. Discuss natural resources, asking critical questions.

4. Show pictures of the mines in the late 1800s.

5. Explain the process of extracting ore from the land.

6. Ask "What happens when the ore runs out?"

7. Discuss this further with the iron range as an example of what happens.

8. Hand out taconite information and read as a class.

9. Talk of what taconite is and how this has replaced mining.

10. Explain what taconite is doing for the area.

11. Have the children think of other ways the iron range can try to revive itself. Do this in groups and then share as a class.

12. Talk about tourism and wrap up.

Assessment:

1. In groups, have students think of ways this area can revive itself.
2. Have them explain why area change economically.
3. Have the students list what happens when a natural resource is used up.
4. Have the students explain what "economy" means in their own words.
5. Have the students apply what they have learned to their town by being able to list what gives people jobs in their area. Are their any natural resources that are found near by? Is it a tourist town? Factories? Etc.

2. Evaluating information

No doubt, if you use the Internet for classroom instruction, you will have the need to evaluate information for classroom use. The following two sources address the use of medicinal herbs.

- "1ST HERBS (http://www.1st-herbs.com/)
- "Algy's Herb Page"(http://www.algy.com/herb/medcat.html)

Survey these two sources and apply the criteria for evaluating Internet information that appeared in this chapter to determine which of these two sites you would use if you were to actually have students learn how they could use herbs in a medicinal manner.

3. Filtering information

Table 18 is a frame addressing the embargo sanctions placed upon Iraq as a result of the invasion of Kuwait. Scan the article "West Likely to Keep Pressure, Sanctions, on Iraq" (http://www2.nando.net/newsroom/ntn/world/082595/world154t_side2.html), and the article "Campaign Against Sanctions on Iraq" (http://www.cam.ac.uk/CambUniv/Societies/casi/) and complete the frame.

	Basis of position on embargo	Position on economic effects of embargo	Position on how embargo affects Iraqi people
CASI			
Governments of U.S. and Great Britain			

Table 18: Effects of Iraqi Embargo.

NOTES

1. C. K. West, J. A. Farmer, and P. M. Wolff, *Instructional design: Implications from cognitive science* (Englewood Cliffs, NJ: Prentice-Hall, 1991).

2. J. R. Anderson, *Cognitive psychology and its implications* (New York: Freeman, 1985).

3. See note 1.

4. T. Nelson, "Replacing the printed word: A complete literary system," ed. S. H. Lavington, *Proceedings IFIP Congress 1980* (North-Holland, 1980) 1013-1023.

5. G. P. Landow, *Hypertext: The convergence of contemporary critical theory and technology* (Baltimore: The Johns Hopkins University Press, 1993).

6. Ryder and Graves, *Reading and learning in content areas* (Englewood Cliffs, NJ: Prentice-Hall, 1994).

7. L. B. Resnick, *Education and learning to think* (Washington, DC: National Academy Press, 1987).

8. I. V. S. Mullis, E. H. Owen, and G. W. Phillips, *America's challenge: Accelerating academic achievement, a summary of findings from 20 years of NAEP* (Princeton, NJ: Educational Testing Service, 1990).

9. G. A. Miller, "The magical number seven plus or minus two: Some limits on our capacity for processing information," *Psychological Review 63* (1956): 81-96.

10. William Katz, "The reference process," *Introduction to reference work,* vol. 1, Basic Information Sources, 6th ed. (New York: McGraw-Hill, 1992).

11. J. Nielsen, *Multimedia and hypertext: The Internet and beyond* (Cambridge, MA: Academic Press, 1995).

12. R. H. Trigg, "Guided tours and tabletops: Tools for communicating in a hypertext environment," *ACM Trans. Office Information Systems 6*, 4 (October 1988): 398-414.

13. P. Duchastel, "Towards methodologies for building knowledge-based instructional systems," *Instructional Science 20*, 5-6 (1992): 349-359.

14. D. Jonassen, "Objectivism versus constructivism: Do we need a new philosophical paradigm?" *Instructional Technology, Research and Development 39*, 3 (1992): 5-14.

15. R. E. Mayer, "Twenty-five years of research on advance organizers," *Instructional Science 8* (1984): 133-169.

16. L. S. Kalkstein and K. M. Valimont, "Climate effects on human health," *Potential effects of future climate changes on forests and vegetation, agriculture, water resources, and human health*, EPA Science and Advisory Committee Monograph no. 25389

(Washington, D.C.: U.S. Environmental Protection Agency, 1987), 122-152.

Chapter 4 — Creating information on the Internet

Overview

This chapter explains the basics of creating information on the World Wide Web (Figure 55) using HTML. Just as a painter needs knowledge of brushes and paints, someone wishing to create Internet content should posses a basic knowledge of the tools of the trade. This chapter includes the following:

- an explanation of the "language" of the WWW—HTML (HyperText Markup Language),

- a brief tutorial on basic HTML,

- examples of Macintosh, Windows, and UNIX software tools for manipulating HTML and how to get your HTML creation or home page on the WWW, and

- a strategy for creating and viewing HTML with limited or no WWW access.

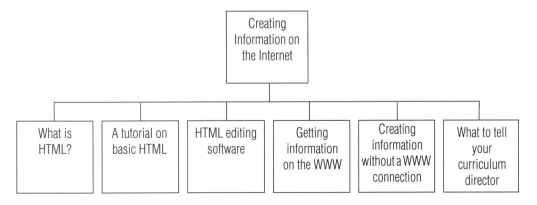

Figure 55: Chapter 4 concept map.

WHAT IS **HTML?**

During our Internet classes we found that students were not satisfied with just browsing the WWW—they wanted to create information on the Web. At first we actually discouraged our students because we didn't want to spend a lot of class time teaching them HTML (HyperText Markup Language), the arcane language of the WWW. We thought students needed some computer programming experience so we tried to steer them away from using HTML. In spite of these misguided efforts, our classes were eager to learn and had little trouble using HTML to make their own WWW pages (often called "home pages"). To their credit, our students produced some surprising results.

HTML is a language that uses "tags" to describe how to format text on the WWW. For example, <H1> and <H2> are HTML tags that stand for "Heading 1" and "Heading 2," respectively. Text that follows an <H1> tag would be very large, like the title of this chapter, "Creating information on the Internet." Text that follows an <H2> tag would be somewhat smaller, like the "What is HTML?" title at the start of this section. Other HTML tags can be used to make text bold, create lists and tables, add color, display pictures, sounds, and movies, and make hypertext links.

Technically, HTML is an **SGML** (Standard Generalized Markup Language) DTD (Document Type Definition). Yes, Virginia, there are a lot of acronyms. SGML and HTML solve a problem that computers created—the exchange of electronic documents between different computers and different computer programs.

Imagine this: you and a colleague are working together on a proposal for a major curriculum project which has to follow strict formatting and style guidelines. Also, you must submit a diskette with the electronic version of your proposal. It's a large project with a fast approaching deadline—Friday—so you and your partner split up the work. On Thursday, both of you finish. The sections of the proposal each of you has completed must now be combined into one polished piece. Your colleague entered her portion of the project on her PC. She used a program called SuperWord 4.0 because it was ideal for creating a proposal to the exacting requirements. However, you used a different word processor—UltraWord 3.5. When you try to electronically combine her SuperWord file into yours, it doesn't work. A message about "Incompatible file type" flashes on your screen. You keep trying, but nothing works and the file is far too large and complex to reenter on your computer. You panic. It's noon on Thursday and the completed proposal must be sent by no later than 5 p.m. However, after a frantic phone call to your partner, she assures you that her SuperWord program can read any type of file. After you race over to her house, she confidently opens her part of the proposal in SuperWord and then tries importing your UltraWord file. "It'll just be a minute," she says. Then her computer beeps and displays the message, "Cannot open this UltraWord 3.5 document. An UltraWord 3.5 filter will be available in the next SuperWord release." You both panic. It's 3:30 p.m. and there's no time to retype. Hoping for the best, you submit both of your diskettes.

Although this situation may not be typical, if you work with computers, you probably know that exchanging electronic documents can often be difficult and frustrating. Portable ASCII (i.e., plain text) documents can be made by many word processors, but ASCII documents are limited to using characters and numbers. All formatting information—like bolding, different fonts, and headings—is lost.

SGML was created to solve the document interchange problem. It is a metalanguage that is used to describe *how* text will be displayed. In a sense, SGML and HTML are used to "program" how text will appear. Because SGML is also an established standard, any computer program has the capability to read and display any SGML document, unlike SuperWord (or almost all word processors) whose files are created using a proprietary coding scheme that only another SuperWord program can read. So it doesn't matter if an HTML document is written on a UNIX, Macintosh, or Windows computer. It also doesn't matter what kind of software is used to create HTML.

A TUTORIAL ON BASIC **HTML**

Though there are over fifty HTML tags available,[1] a respectable home page can be created using just a few of these. However, to complicate matters, there are different versions of HTML. That is, some HTML tags may not be understood by all WWW browsers. For example, the <BLINK> tag was invented by Netscape Communications to work with their browser, but the NCSA Mosaic browser doesn't recognize it. Although this should be of little concern if you're just creating simple home pages, it is an issue if you want to create something more complex with HTML. This potential incompatibility is addressed under the topic "HTML editing software" later in this chapter.

Besides a plethora of books on using HTML, there are a number of resources on the World Wide Web available for free. A good starting point is the HTML Writers Guild (http://www.synet.net/hwg) (Figure 56).

To demonstrate HTML, we'll reverse engineer, or take apart, a home page (Figure 57) to show how some of the common HTML tags are used.

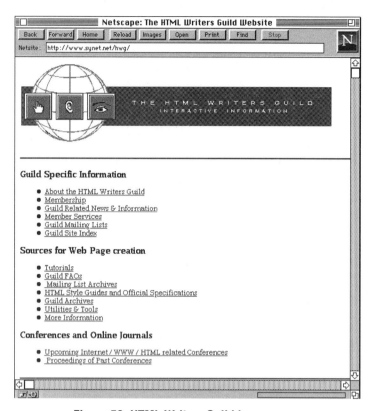

Figure 56: HTML Writers Guild home page.

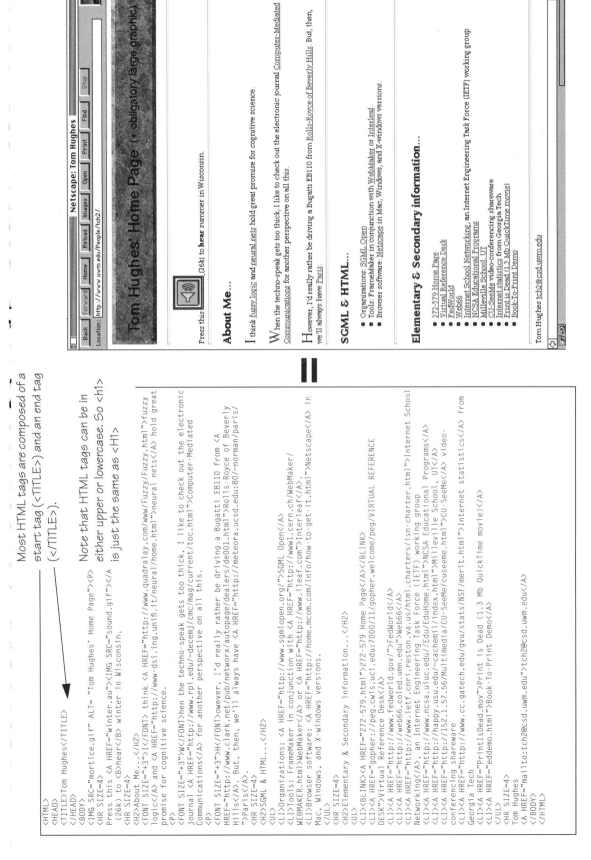

Figure 57: HTML code (left) and how it looks on a WWW browser (right).

Step 1 — Beginnings and endings: <HTML>, <HEAD>, and <BODY> tags

Figure 58 shows how to start and end an HTML document. Note that the tags do not have to be indented in the figure. This is only done for ease of reading.

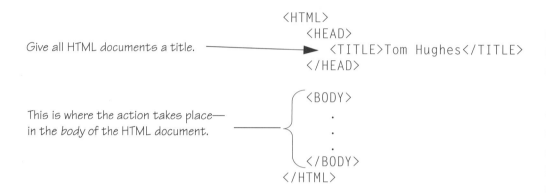

Give all HTML documents a title.

```
<HTML>
    <HEAD>
        <TITLE>Tom Hughes</TITLE>
    </HEAD>
```

This is where the action takes place— in the *body* of the HTML document.

```
    <BODY>
        .
        .
        .
    </BODY>
</HTML>
```

Figure 58: The beginning and end of an HTML document.

Step 2 — In-line graphics: <IMG SRC> tag

Figure 59 shows how to display graphics using the <IMG SRC> tag. Graphics used on a home page are typically GIF files. A GIF file is a special kind of bitmap image format. It is similar to, but not the same as, a Macintosh PICT or a Windows BMP file. A program like Adobe Photoshop can be used to convert images to a GIF format.

Care should be taken not to put very large images on your home page. Most people on the Internet use slow modems and the larger the graphic, the slower it will be displayed.

```
<IMG SRC="mortice.gif"
ALT= "Tom Hughes' Home
Page">
```

This HTML code displays a graphic called "mortice.gif." If someone is using a WWW browser that cannot show graphics,[2] then the phrase "Tom Hughes' Home Page" will appear instead.

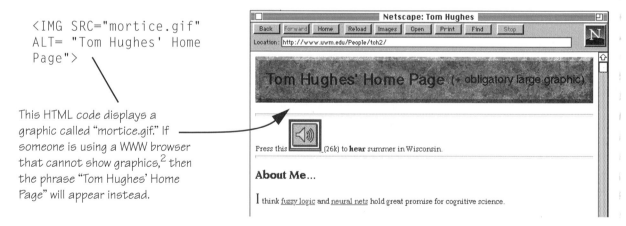

Figure 59: How to display graphics.

Step 3 — Horizontal rules: <HR> tag

A horizontal rule can be used to divide the major sections of a home page. This tag can be used all by itself, like <HR>, or with a number, like <HR SIZE=4> as in Figure 60 to specify the point size (thickness) of the rule.

<HR SIZE=4>

Figure 60: Horizontal rules.

Step 4 — Font size: <FONT SIZE> tag

Though not really basic HTML, <FONT SIZE> is a nifty way to make large initial letters (Figure 61) to emphasize text.

The large letters at the beginning of
each of the three sentences below were
created using the following HTML code:

```
<FONT SIZE="+3">I</FONT>
<FONT SIZE="+3">W</FONT>
<FONT SIZE="+3">H</FONT>
```

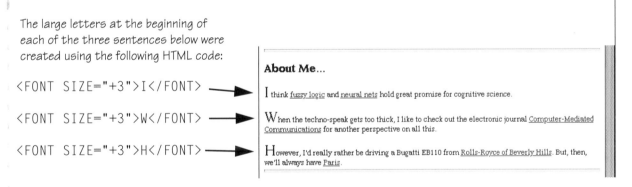

Make sure to place the end tag </FONT> after
each letter. Otherwise, the text will remain large.

Figure 61: Using the <FONT SIZE> tag.

Step 5 — Hypertext links: <A> tag

The anchor, or <A> tag, is usually used to create links from your home page to other places on the WWW. However, links can be made from one part to another part of a home page. Anchor links are called hypertext, the fundamental navigational method of the World Wide Web. Hypertext links can be designated by either underlined text (Figure 62) or a graphic (Figure 63). When you click on the underlined text or graphic, the WWW browser goes to the location specified in the hypertext link.

In order to get to the location, a "path" is specified. For example, in Figure 62, the path to the hypertext link "fuzzy logic" is:

www.quadralay.com/www/Fuzzy/Fuzzy.html.

Note: in paths, capitalization <u>does</u> matter.

The first part, *www.quadralay.com*, is the main address of Quadralay Corporation's WWW site. The *www* and *Fuzzy* are directories (or folders, for you Macintosh users). The last part of the path, *Fuzzy.html*, is the actual file that contains the HTML code for the fuzzy logic home page.

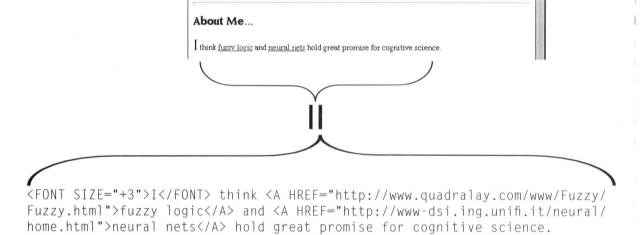

Figure 62: A hypertext link made with text.

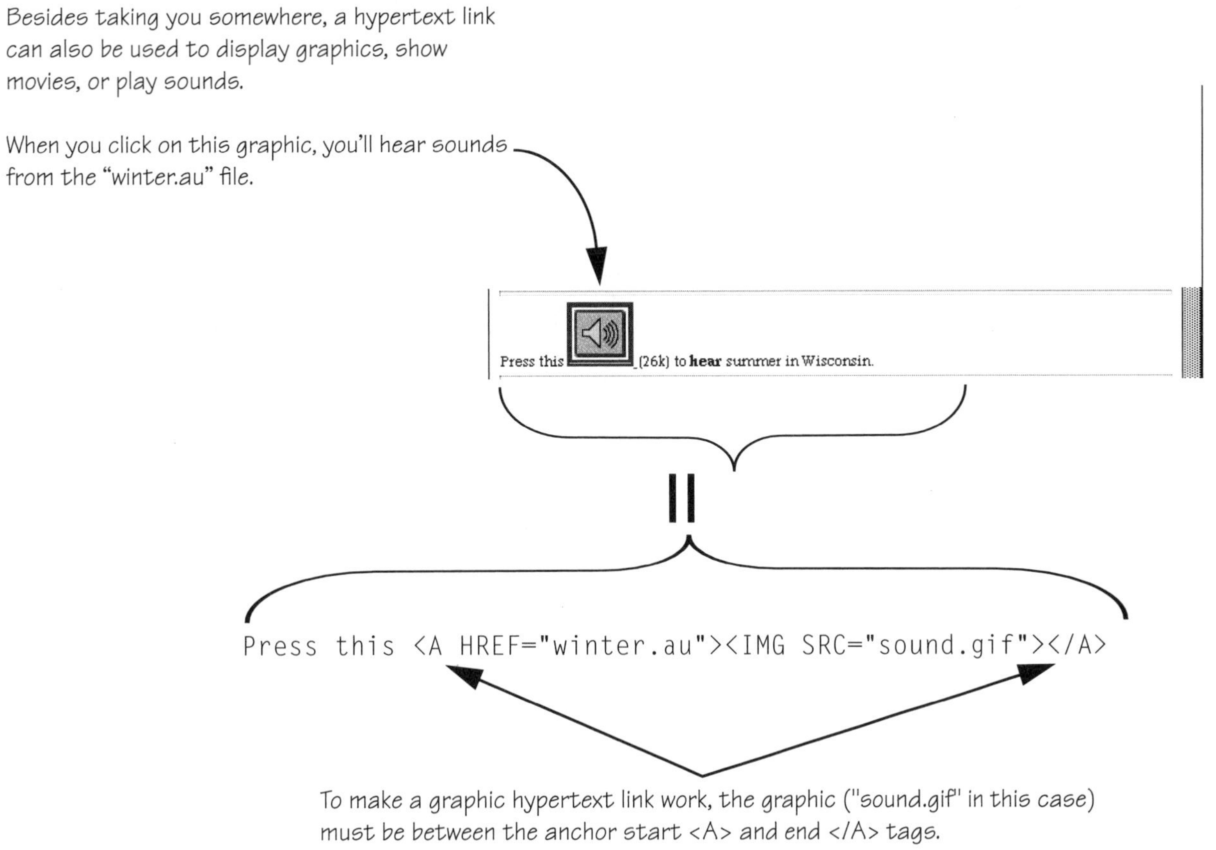

Besides taking you somewhere, a hypertext link
can also be used to display graphics, show
movies, or play sounds.

When you click on this graphic, you'll hear sounds
from the "winter.au" file.

Press this [🔊] _____ (26k) to **hear** summer in Wisconsin.

=

Press this <A HREF="winter.au"><IMG SRC="sound.gif"></A>

To make a graphic hypertext link work, the graphic ("sound.gif" in this case)
must be between the anchor start <A> and end </A> tags.

Figure 63: A hypertext link made with a graphic.

Step 6 — Headlines: <H1>, <H2>, <H3>, <H4>, <H5>, and <H6> tags

Headlines come in six levels or sizes with <H1> the largest and <H6> the smallest. All the headlines used in our sample home page are <H2> (Figure 64).

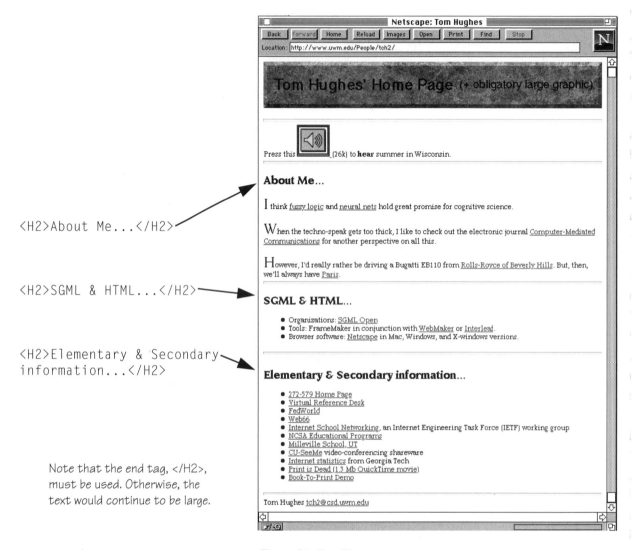

<H2>About Me...</H2>

<H2>SGML & HTML...</H2>

<H2>Elementary & Secondary information...</H2>

Note that the end tag, </H2>, must be used. Otherwise, the text would continue to be large.

Figure 64: Headlines.

Step 7 — Lists: <UL>, <OL>, and <LI> tags

HTML can create bulleted (or unordered, Figure 65) and numbered (or ordered, Figure 66) lists with the <UL> and <OL> tags, respectively. Each item in either an unordered or ordered list must start with the <LI> tag. An </LI> end tag is not necessary after each list item. However, at the end of the *entire* list, an end tag (</UL> or </OL>) must be included.

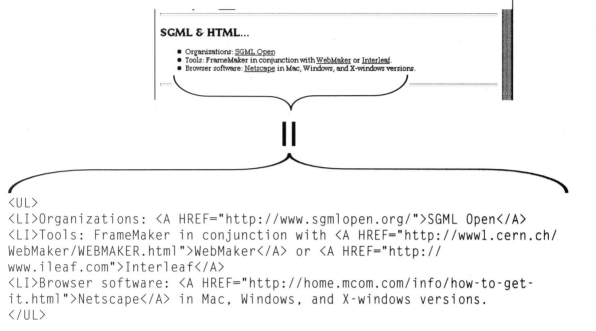

```
<UL>
<LI>Organizations: <A HREF="http://www.sgmlopen.org/">SGML Open</A>
<LI>Tools: FrameMaker in conjunction with <A HREF="http://www1.cern.ch/
WebMaker/WEBMAKER.html">WebMaker</A> or <A HREF="http://
www.ileaf.com">Interleaf</A>
<LI>Browser software: <A HREF="http://home.mcom.com/info/how-to-get-
it.html">Netscape</A> in Mac, Windows, and X-windows versions.
</UL>
```

Figure 65: Unordered list.

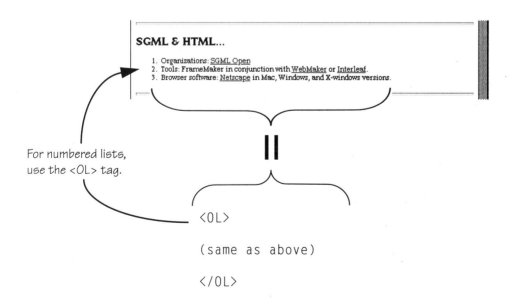

For numbered lists, use the <OL> tag.

```
<OL>

(same as above)

</OL>
```

Figure 66: Ordered list.

Step 8 — Automatic e-mailing: mailto tag

Though technically not an HTML tag, mailto can be used along with an anchor tag to create a mechanism by which people can e-mail you directly from your home page (Figure 67).

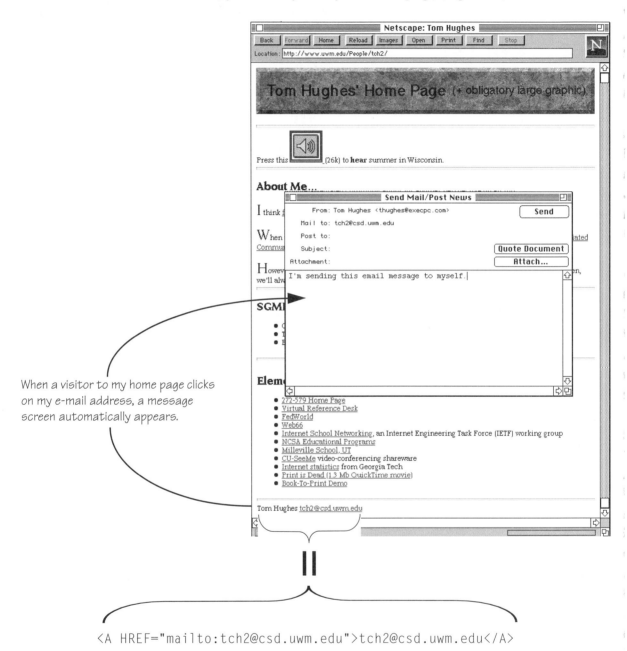

When a visitor to my home page clicks on my e-mail address, a message screen automatically appears.

```
<A HREF="mailto:tch2@csd.uwm.edu">tch2@csd.uwm.edu</A>
```

Figure 67: Automatic e-mailing.

HTML EDITING SOFTWARE

The tools you ultimately use to create Internet content will probably come down to what your school can afford. We think that the best software requires little or no knowledge of HTML to use. Programs like Adobe PageMill and Claris Home Page fall into this category because each uses a WYSIWYG (What You See Is What You Get) approach to creating Internet content. However, even though these programs are inexpensive, the cost quickly escalates if you need a copy for each student. This means that you may be forced to rely on Internet freeware or shareware in order to generate material for your Net.

HTML can be written with an ordinary word processor or with an intelligent "parser" program that can check for errors in your HTML code. What is used depends on your needs. If you're just experimenting, then an ordinary word processor capable of outputting an ASCII (i.e., plain text) file is all that's necessary. However, if you envision yourself using HTML on a regular basis, then more powerful HTML tools are available.

The different versions of HTML

Though HTML is standardized, there are different "flavors" of it. Currently, there are three versions of HTML:

1. Official HTML—maintained by the IETF (Internet Engineering Task Force),

2. Netscape HTML—the version of HTML used in the Netscape Navigator browser, and

3. Microsoft HTML—the version of HTML used in Microsoft's Internet Explorer browser.

Because the driving force of the Internet is now its commercial application, rivals Netscape and Microsoft have not fully cooperated on standardizing HTML. This is likely to continue and has implications for someone creating HTML.[3] Which version should be used? Is the "official" IETF version of HTML always the best choice? We can only suggest that you consider *how* you will use the HTML you create. For example, if students will be using HTML for short-term projects such as simple home pages, there is little need for a rigorous approach. In this case any version of HTML will do because only very basic HTML tags would be used. On the other hand, if students will be part of an ongoing HTML project like a WWW school newspaper, then more care should be taken. However, to avoid devoting too much time to teaching HTML, the use of sophisticated HTML editing software, such as SoftQuad's HoTMetaL Pro (http://www.sq.com), should be considered.

Basic HTML software

Basic editing software is usually not able to check for errors in HTML syntax. The burden of producing "correct" HTML is on the writer. However, basic is not the same as crude. There is a wide spectrum of software in this category that ranges from word processors to WYSIWYG HTML editors. Some of this software is also available for little or no cost on the WWW.

Word processors

In most cases, when word processing software is used to create HTML, the HTML is written offline (i.e., when you're not on the Internet) and moved to the WWW after it's finished. If students have limited WWW access, this is a very practical way of writing HTML.

However, HTML can be created online (i.e., when you are on the Internet). For example, because our HTML was destined to be placed on a UNIX computer, we wrote it using emacs (Figure 68), a UNIX word processor. On our home PCs we ran a WWW browser at the same time we used emacs to create the HTML. This allowed us to see the results of our work almost immediately. We would do some editing in emacs and then view the results in Netscape.

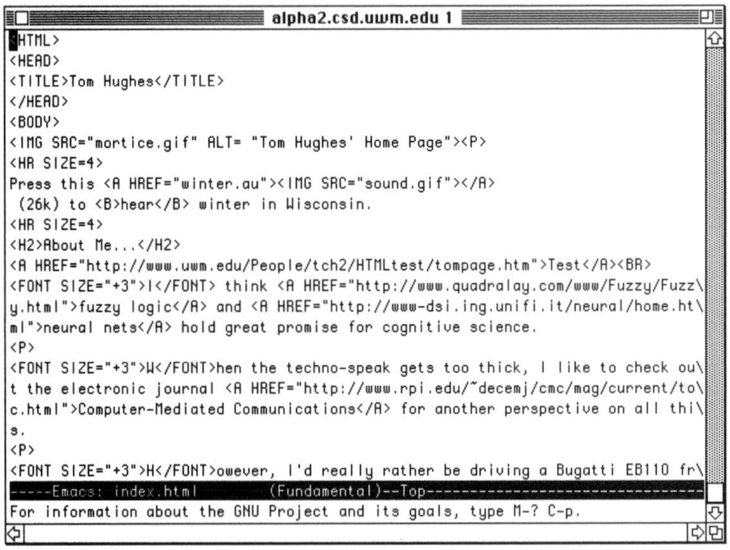

```
┌─□─────────────── alpha2.csd.uwm.edu 1 ───────────────┐
│<HTML>                                                 │
│<HEAD>                                                 │
│<TITLE>Tom Hughes</TITLE>                              │
│</HEAD>                                                │
│<BODY>                                                 │
│<IMG SRC="mortice.gif" ALT= " Tom Hughes' Home Page"><P>│
│<HR SIZE=4>                                            │
│Press this <A HREF="winter.au"><IMG SRC="sound.gif"></A>│
│ (26k) to <B>hear</B> winter in Wisconsin.            │
│<HR SIZE=4>                                            │
│<H2>About Me...</H2>                                   │
│<A HREF="http://www.uwm.edu/People/tch2/HTMLtest/tompage.htm">Test</A><BR>│
│<FONT SIZE="+3">I</FONT> think <A HREF="http://www.quadralay.com/www/Fuzzy/Fuzz\│
│y.html">fuzzy logic</A> and <A HREF="http://www-dsi.ing.unifi.it/neural/home.ht\│
│ml">neural nets</A> hold great promise for cognitive science.│
│<P>                                                    │
│<FONT SIZE="+3">W</FONT>hen the techno-speak gets too thick, I like to check ou\│
│t the electronic journal <A HREF="http://www.rpi.edu/~decemj/cmc/mag/current/to\│
│c.html">Computer-Mediated Communications</A> for another perspective on all thi\│
│s.                                                     │
│<P>                                                    │
│<FONT SIZE="+3">H</FONT>owever, I'd really rather be driving a Bugatti EB110 fr\│
│-----Emacs: index.html       (Fundamental)--Top-----------------------------│
│For information about the GNU Project and its goals, type M-? C-p.│
└───────────────────────────────────────────────────────┘
```

Figure 68: emacs: a UNIX word processor.

PC word processors, like Microsoft Word, are probably the most suitable solutions for offline HTML editing. Also, many word processing and desktop publishing programs like PageMaker, QuarkXPress, and FrameMaker are incorporating HTML functions. For example, Microsoft Word allows any document to be saved as HTML (Figure 69).

Dedicated HTML editors

Special-purpose software has arisen that is devoted specifically

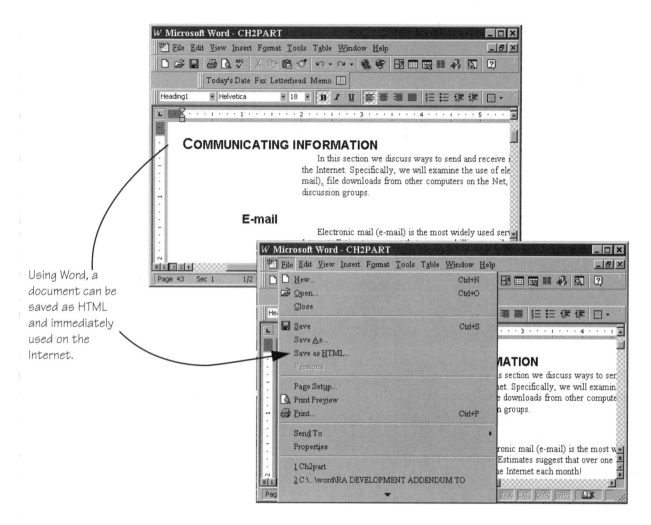

Using Word, a document can be saved as HTML and immediately used on the Internet.

Figure 69: Microsoft Word can save documents as HTML.

to HTML. Unlike word processors, which are multifunctional and expensive, HTML editors are usually limited to creating and editing HTML and usually don't cost much. In other words, most HTML editors would make poor word processors. There are many dedicated HTML editors and most are either free or inexpensive (unlike word processors). Though only a few of these are presented here, we hope our examples are typical of an ease-of-use trend.

Web Weaver (http://www.northnet.org/best) and HotDog (http://www.sausage.com/) are two programs that seem to represent the current trend in dedicated HTML editors: Both have special HTML toolbars to assist editing, and both use WWW browsers to preview HTML code. Web Weaver (Figure 70) is a Macintosh application and HotDog (Figure 71) is a Windows program.

However, the winner for ease of use must go to WEB Wizard (http://www.halcyon.com/artamedia/webwizard) for Windows (Figures 72, 73, and 74). In eight steps this program creates a home page for you using a series of "interview" notecards. Though limited in power, this program is a blessing for HTML novices or those with little or no interest in learning the intricacies of HTML.

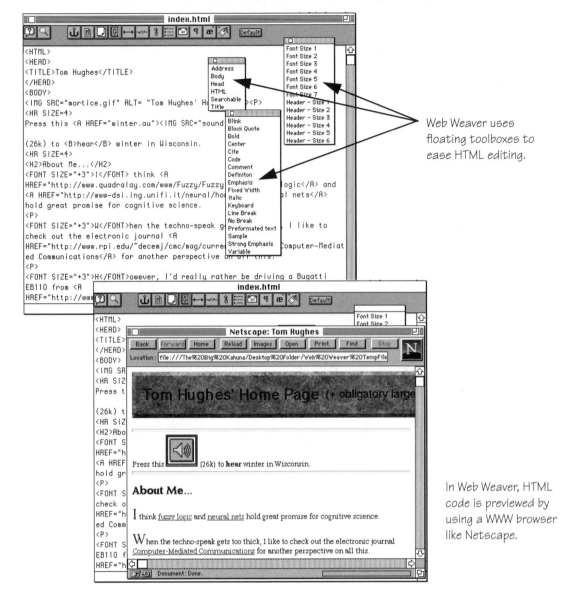

Web Weaver uses floating toolboxes to ease HTML editing.

In Web Weaver, HTML code is previewed by using a WWW browser like Netscape.

Figure 70: Web Weaver HTML editor (Macintosh).

Though WEB Wizard is incredibly user-friendly, its lack of power restricts its use. That is, if you wish to make something more than a very basic home page, then a more complex HTML editor has to be used—and powerful software need not be synonymous with difficult software.

Intuitive, WYSIWYG software is coming on the market that will make writing HTML as easy as editing text in today's word processors. Adobe's PageMill (http://www.adobe.com) (Figure 75) is an example of software designed to create WWW information much like PageMaker is used for desktop publishing.

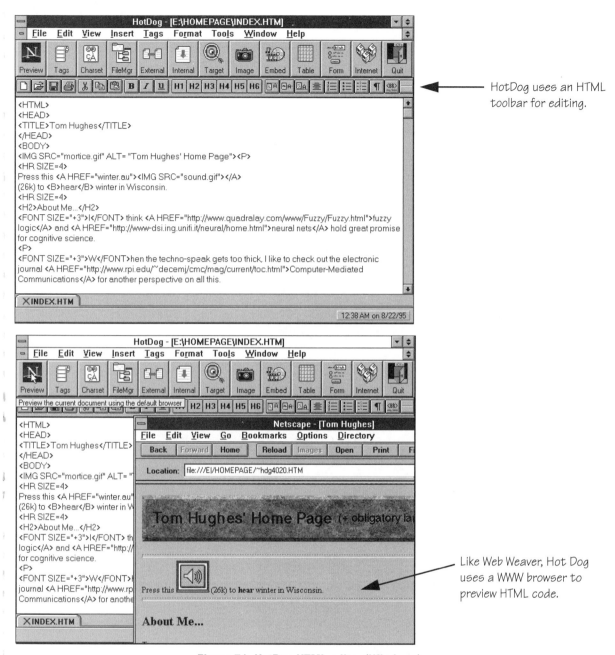

HotDog uses an HTML toolbar for editing.

Like Web Weaver, Hot Dog uses a WWW browser to preview HTML code.

Figure 71: HotDog HTML editor (Windows).

Advanced HTML software

Usually software is this category is only recommended if you must generate HTML that conforms to strict standards. This would involve situations in which the HTML will be around for some time (unlike personal home pages) and in which many people may be involved in editing the HTML (again, unlike home pages). Also, this software could be used as an adjunct to computer science classes because HTML shares many characteristics with traditional

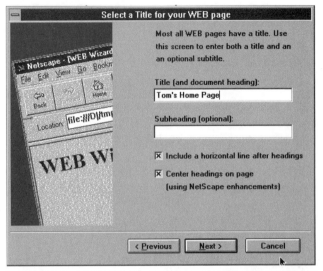

STEP 1 — Give a title to your home page.

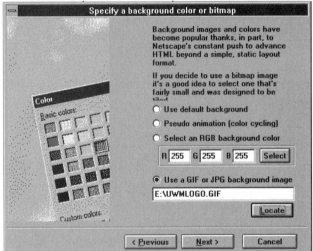

STEP 2 — Use a background color or image.

STEP 3 — Add a graphic.

Figure 72: (Part 1) WEB Wizard's eight-step home page creation process.

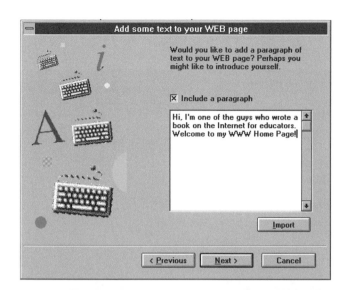

STEP 4 — Add text to your home page.

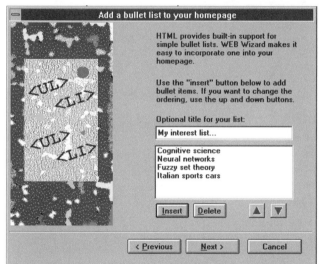

STEP 5 — Create a list.

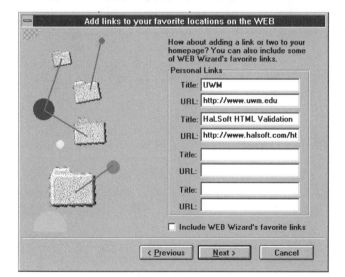

STEP 6 — Add some hypertext links.

Figure 73: (Part 2) WEB Wizard's eight-step home page creation process.

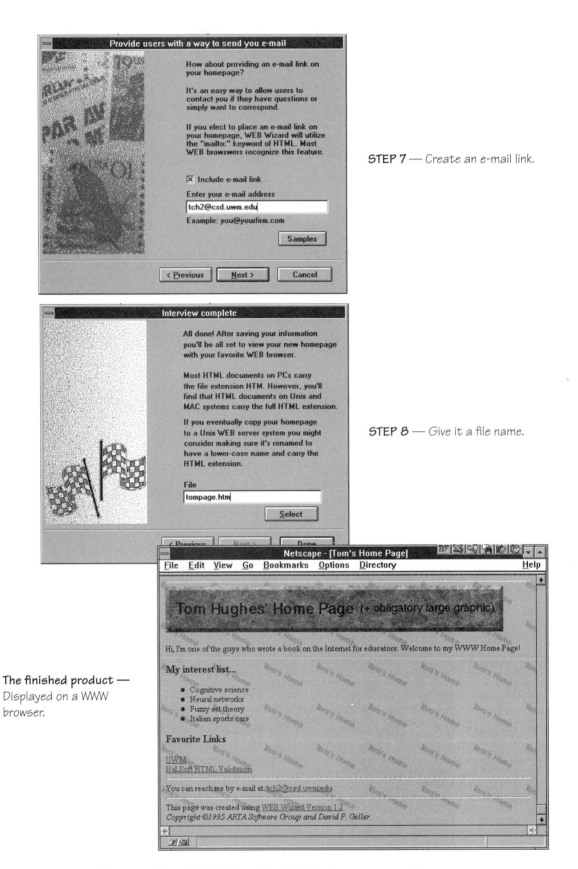

STEP 7 — *Create an e-mail link.*

STEP 8 — *Give it a file name.*

The finished product — Displayed on a WWW browser.

Figure 74: (Part 3) WEB Wizard's eight-step home page creation process.

PageMill allows "drag-and-drop" editing of a home page.
That is, graphics and text can be easily manipulated to
create a WWW site. No knowledge of HTML tags is required.

A graphic can be edited by
just clicking on it.

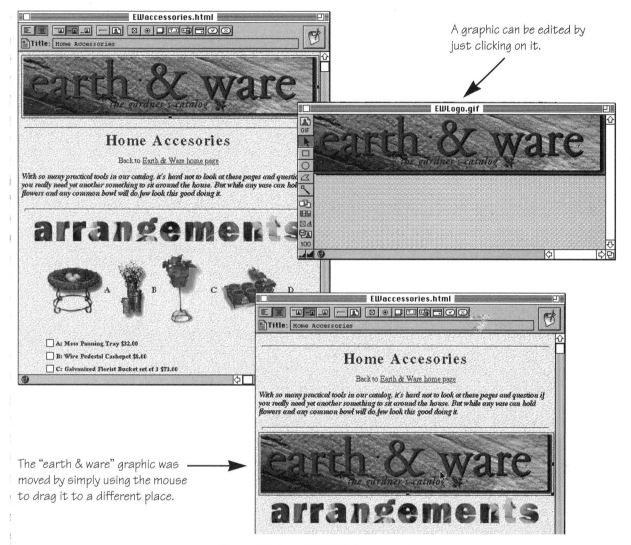

The "earth & ware" graphic was
moved by simply using the mouse
to drag it to a different place.

Figure 75: PageMill HTML software.

computer programming languages.

Though there is no shortage of basic HTML software, this cannot
be said of the advanced software. There just isn't much out there.
This may be because HTML is relatively easy to learn,[4] so there
isn't that much of a demand.

SoftQuad's HoTMetaL Pro (http://www.sq.com) is an HTML
parser available for both Macintosh and Windows (Figure 76). While
in no way as easy as the WEB Wizard software, HoTMetaL Pro
automates much of the editing process. It also validates the
resulting HTML code far more rigorously than any of the previously
mentioned HTML editors.

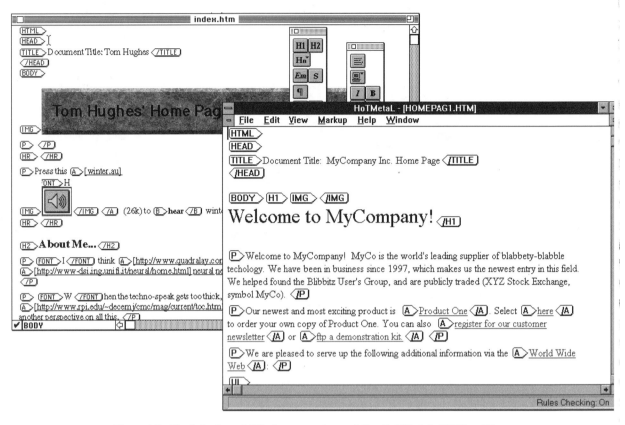

Figure 76: Macintosh and Windows versions of the HoTMetaL HTML editor.

GETTING INFORMATION ON THE INTERNET

In order for the world to see HTML, it will have to be transferred to a World Wide Web server. This is a computer with WWW access to the Internet. Usually this will be the computer of your Internet service provider.

Unless you create HTML directly on your service provider's computer (e.g., with emacs software), the most typical way of moving HTML code from someone's PC to a WWW server is with a file transfer protocol. Remember that you will also have to move any graphic, sound, or movie files that your HTML code uses. (However, if you're fortunate enough to live or work close to your service provider, then "sneaker net" may be more practical. That is, you may want to just walk over with a diskette of your HTML.) Xmodem, Kermit, and ftp are common transfer protocols. The first two protocols will work if you have a "shell" Internet connection.[5] The last method, ftp, works if you have a LAN or PPP connection to the Internet. Because you will probably want more than shell access to the Internet, we'll only consider ftp.

On the Windows side, the multifunctional program WinQVT (Figures 77 and 78) includes ftp as well as telnet and e-mail support. For the Macintosh, a program called Fetch (http://

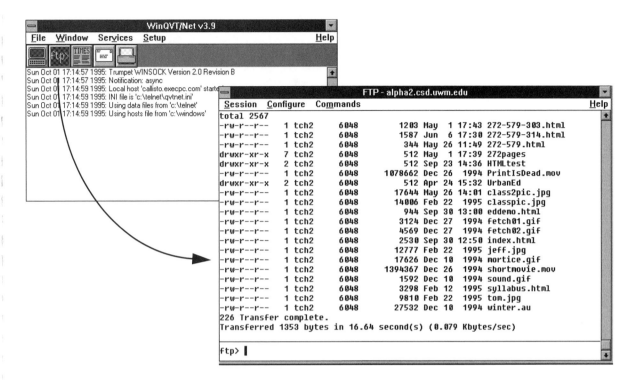

Figure 77: WinQVT's ftp function.

www.dartmouth.edu/pages/softdev/fetch.html) (Figure 79) offers a more intuitive approach to ftp. Though ftp is a UNIX process, Fetch takes the UNIX "out" of ftp and replaces it with a much friendlier Macintosh interface.

Because many programs operate like WinQVT, it will be used to demonstrate an ftp file transfer. In this example, a graphic file titled "mortice.gif" will be sent from our PC to our Internet service provider.

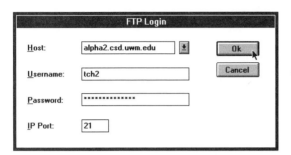

First, a LAN or PPP connection is opened to an Internet service provider.

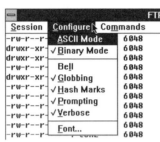

Second, you need to set the type of file you're sending—either **ASCII** or **Binary**. Use **ASCII** to send text files, and select **Binary** for everything else.

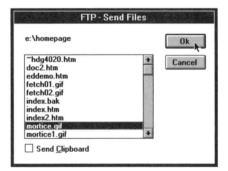

Third, on your PC, locate the file you're going to send, **mortice.gif**.

Finally, WinQVT transfers **mortice.gif** to your Internet account.

```
                              FTP - alpha2.csd.uwm.edu
Session   Configure   Commands                                            Help
-rw-r--r--    1 tch2      6048          2530 Sep 30 12:50 index.html
-rw-r--r--    1 tch2      6048         12777 Feb 22  1995 jeff.jpg
-rw-r--r--    1 tch2      6048         17626 Dec 10  1994 mortice.gif
-rw-r--r--    1 tch2      6048       1394367 Dec 26  1994 shortmovie.mov
-rw-r--r--    1 tch2      6048          1592 Dec 10  1994 sound.gif
-rw-r--r--    1 tch2      6048          3298 Feb 12  1995 syllabus.html
-rw-r--r--    1 tch2      6048          9810 Feb 22  1995 tom.jpg
-rw-r--r--    1 tch2      6048         27532 Dec 10  1994 winter.au
226 Transfer complete.
Transferred 1353 bytes in 16.64 second(s) (0.079 Kbytes/sec)
?Invalid command (mv)
> binary
200 Type set to I.
> lcd e:/homepage
Local directory now e:\homepage
> send mortice.gif
200 Type set to I.
200 PORT command successful.
150 Opening BINARY mode data connection for mortice.gif.
##
226 Transfer complete.
remote file: mortice.gif  local file: mortice.gif
Transferred 17626 bytes in 2.53 second(s) (6.814 Kbytes/sec)

ftp> |
```

Figure 78: Using WinQVT's ftp function to send a file.

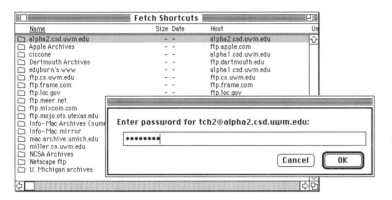

Like WinQVT, the first thing you do with Fetch is open a connection to your Internet service provider.

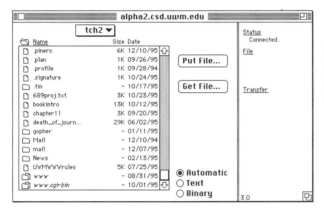

However, unlike WinQVT, Fetch uses a distinctly Macintosh interface. For example, UNIX directories are shown as Macintosh folders.

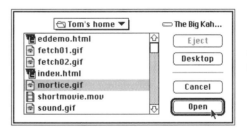

A file is ftp'd by selecting it from your Macintosh.

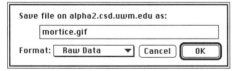

However, the last step is tricky because a Macintosh stores its files differently than other PCs.[6] When you use Fetch to upload a file, select the "Raw Data" Format for each file you upload unless the file you're uploading is plain text.

Figure 79: Using Fetch for ftp.

CREATING INFORMATION WITHOUT AN INTERNET CONNECTION

Even without Internet access, it's possible to create and examine a WWW site. The "local" or "open file" mode of a WWW browser can be used to view HTML code and images which are stored on your computer. This method of viewing a WWW site is called local HTML, and it has some limitations:

- In order to see the local WWW site on a particular computer, all the HTML code, image, sound, and so on files must be stored on that computer. Even if your PC was connected to a network, the other computers on the network would not be able to access the local HTML code stored on your machine. If someone else wished to see your home page on *their* PC, all the files used to create your local home page (i.e., HTML code, graphics, sounds, movies, etc.) would need to be copied to their computer.

- With local HTML, links to WWW sites *on the Internet* will not function. For example, if a link to the White House (http://www.whitehouse.gov) is selected from your local HTML file, your WWW browser will not be able to connect to the White House. (Unless, of course, your computer has Internet access. But we're assuming it doesn't.)

Despite these limitations, local HTML has some practical advantages, especially for schools.

- No Internet access is necessary. In an era of tight budgets, this is especially important.

- Assigning HTML homework is possible. Projects need not be confined to the school. Though a student would still need a home computer, Internet access would be optional.

Although local HTML is no substitute for real Internet access, it can be used successfully for small projects and in situations where only limited Internet access is possible.

A local HTML example

Local HTML can be created by either writing it from scratch on your PC or downloading existing HTML files from the WWW. If you have no Internet access at all, then you must select the former. This is how students would probably make local HTML at home. However, even with limited connectivity, it's possible to create a mini-Internet on your personal computer by downloading HTML files from the World Wide Web. In fact, given enough hard disk space, you could download most of the WWW to your computer! Although this is impractical, copying an HTML tutorial from the Internet and making it into local HTML is a very efficient use.

The files for the home page in Figure 57 are located on a UNIX computer (Figure 80). Because the UNIX machine is connected to the Internet and uses special WWW server software, these home page files can be accessed and viewed by anyone with Internet access and a WWW browser.

```
                        alpha2.csd.uwm.edu 1

(alpha2) 13: ls -l
total 2567
-rw-r--r--    1 tch2      6048        1203 May  1 17:43 272-579-303.html
-rw-r--r--    1 tch2      6048        1587 Jun  6 17:30 272-579-314.html
-rw-r--r--    1 tch2      6048         344 May 26 11:49 272-579.html
drwxr-xr-x    7 tch2      6048         512 May  1 17:39 272pages/
drwxr-xr-x    2 tch2      6048         512 Sep 23 14:36 HTMLtest/
-rw-r--r--    1 tch2      6048     1078662 Dec 26  1994 PrintIsDead.mov
drwxr-xr-x    2 tch2      6048         512 Apr 24 15:32 UrbanEd/
-rw-r--r--    1 tch2      6048       17644 May 26 14:01 class2pic.jpg
-rw-r--r--    1 tch2      6048       14006 Feb 22  1995 classpic.jpg
-rw-r--r--    1 tch2      6048         944 Sep 30 13:00 eddemo.html
-rw-r--r--    1 tch2      6048        3124 Dec 27  1994 fetch01.gif
-rw-r--r--    1 tch2      6048        4569 Dec 27  1994 fetch02.gif
-rw-r--r--    1 tch2      6048        2530 Sep 30 12:50 index.html
-rw-r--r--    1 tch2      6048       12777 Feb 22  1995 jeff.jpg
-rw-r--r--    1 tch2      6048       17626 Dec 10  1994 mortice.gif
-rw-r--r--    1 tch2      6048     1394367 Dec 26  1994 shortmovie.mov
-rw-r--r--    1 tch2      6048        1592 Dec 10  1994 sound.gif
-rw-r--r--    1 tch2      6048        3298 Feb 12  1995 syllabus.html
-rw-r--r--    1 tch2      6048        9810 Feb 22  1995 tom.jpg
-rw-r--r--    1 tch2      6048       27532 Dec 10  1994 winter.au
(alpha2) 14:
```

Figure 80: Home page files on a UNIX computer.

To show that this home page can be recreated—or at least parts of it—using local HTML, the home page files were transferred from the UNIX computer to a Macintosh. Though an ftp program like Fetch could have been used to copy the files, a program called WebWhacker (http://www.ffg.com)(Figure 81), available for Macintosh and Windows, was used because it is specifically designed to create local HTML.

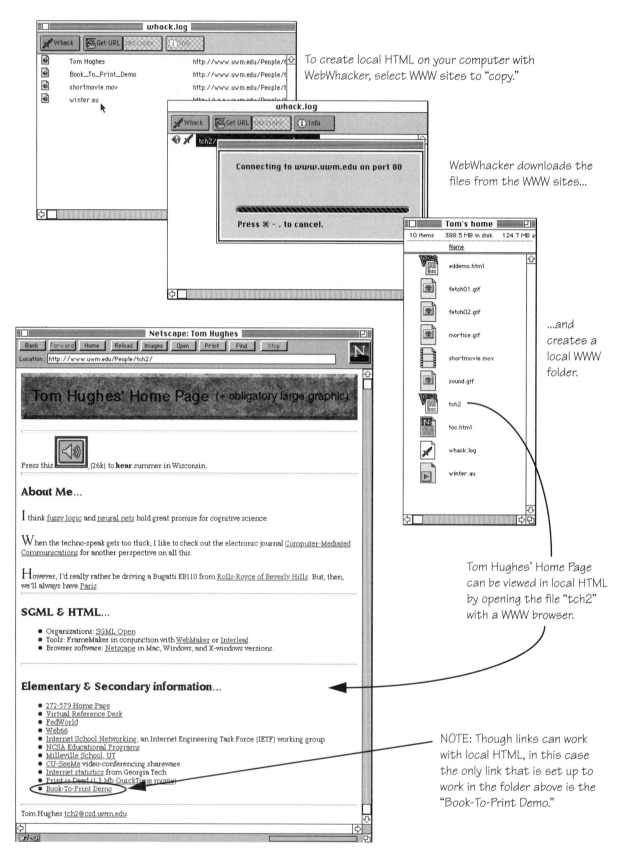

Figure 81: WebWhacker—a program designed to create local HTML.

WHAT TO TELL YOUR CURRICULUM DIRECTOR

We think it's a given that learning HTML for its own sake has little practical or educational value. Expecting students to memorize a bunch of tags like <H1> is certainly a waste of their time, especially considering that software like PageMill, which requires very little knowledge of HTML, is the future of home page creation software. Whereas HTML might make a nifty unit in a computer science class or possibly in a language arts class, the value of HTML is determined by what students can *create* with it, not what they know *about* it.

However, on the other extreme, we are not suggesting that the Internet become the curriculum, but rather that the Internet is a technology that must be meaningfully integrated into the curriculum. Nevertheless, just as the calculator has moved mathematics instruction toward problem solving and away from rote drill, it is reasonable to expect that a similar paradigm shift will occur after the introduction of the Internet.

A constructivist paradigm

Now is a good time to reaffirm our faith in generative learning by listing some basic tenets of constructivist learning[7] and their relationship to creating information on the Internet:

- Students are viewed as thinkers with emerging theories about the world and pursuit of their questions is highly valued.

- Students work primarily in groups.

- Curricular activities rely heavily on primary sources of data and manipulative materials.

- Teachers generally behave in an interactive manner, mediating the environment for students.

- Assessment of student learning is interwoven with teaching and occurs through teacher observations of students at work and through student exhibitions and portfolios.

Information-creating activities that encourage generative learning

The strength of the Internet (and especially a school Intranet) is that it allows anyone with a rudimentary knowledge of HTML to create a personal world—a microworld, a rich environment for learning[8]. With the principles of constructivist learning in mind, here are some suggestions for the type of information schools could create on the Internet:

- Personal Home Pages—Essentially a collage of the self, a student home page adds a new dimension to self-expression in which text, graphics, sounds, and movies can be used to create a public artifact. Though the sheer novelty of using graphics, sounds, and so on should initially motivate students, the excitement is bound to diminish over time. However, even when making Internet movies becomes commonplace for students, they will have a valuable new set of skills and experiences with different modes of communication.

- Multimedia Newspapers—Whereas a home page is typically a solitary endeavor, an online student newspaper requires a cooperative effort. This multimedia newspaper could be similar to the traditional school newspaper or it could be a product of a single class. For example, as part of a biology class studying the environment, results of student investigations into their local environment could be posted (along with pictures) on a Biology home page. This activity might also involve collecting and sharing data from sites around the world and then evaluating the results.

- Online Portfolios—A student's work intended for public display could be archived in an online collection. This portfolio could begin in the primary grades and follow a student through graduation from high school. The portfolio could be used to demonstrate a student's work from all courses, acting as a sort of "Internet across the Curriculum."

- Course Supplements—A WWW site could be made to serve as a resource for a particular class or curricular area. For example, assignments, additional readings, and links to relevant Internet sites could be included at a class site.

- Community Resource—Though not necessarily created by students, students could participate in a community Internet site. Such a site would present information of interest to the immediate area such as local events and activities.

CONCLUDING REMARKS

This chapter has provided a basic tutorial for creating information on the World Wide Web. Specifically, it provided an explanation of HTML, a description of the basic elements of HTML, a description of HTML editing software, how information is placed on the WWW, and how you can create information without a WWW connection. In concluding this chapter we would like to review several important concepts.

HTML is a special markup language that is used to create Internet World Wide Web sites, which are often referred to as home pages. Because HTML follows a standard, home pages can be viewed by any computer that can run WWW browser software. These home pages are a useful means for schools to communicate with students, the community, and for sharing student's learning products to the others on the Internet.

We would also note the ease of constructing a home page. Using ordinary word processors, HTML can be composed in a relatively straightforward manner. As more emphasis is placed on editing software based on WYSIWYG applications, the effort required for HTML composition will be further reduced.

Finally, information-creating activities are suggested that conform to our belief in the generative nature of learning.

ACTIVITIES

1. For younger students

Children in the earlier grades cannot be expected to do their own HTML editing, and teachers will have to do the bulk of the "coding." However, younger children can still use the WWW to display their work whether their project involves text, graphic, or both.

As part of a unit on local insects, each student in one Arizona classroom drew a picture and wrote a brief description of a "dangerous bug" (Figure 82).

The tarantulas are not harmful because they do not sting.

A tarantula is Hairy and has 8 larges and eyes. They eat insects or uthr spiders

Figure 82: A WWW project for younger students.

2. Individual project

Make a home page that can be viewed either on the Internet or in local HTML. The home page should

- contain a brief description of who you are,

- show your understanding of HTML, particularly links, and

- reflect your personal interests by displaying links to WWW sites you find interesting.

If possible, show your creation to other class members and explain the process you went through to create it.

3. Collaborative project

As part of a group or class, design and write a home page on a theme or area of interest. Consider the following examples:

- a resource site in which all group members gather and then present information on a specific area of knowledge (Figure 83),

- a thematic site in which each group member contributes data in a specific area of interest that will be combined under a general topic (Figure 84),

- a Multimedia Newspaper that focuses on either class, local, or national issues. As well as text, the newspaper should be composed of images, sound, and movies (Figure 85).

This HTML tutorial is located at
http://www.eit.com/web/www.guide/

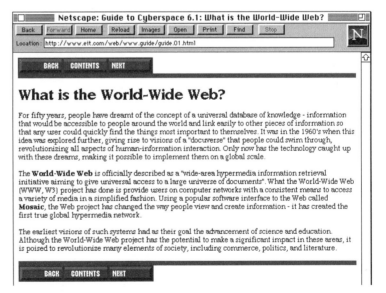

Figure 83: Example of a resource site: an HTML tutorial.

This is part of Madison Middle School 2000's WWW site (http://198.150.8.9)

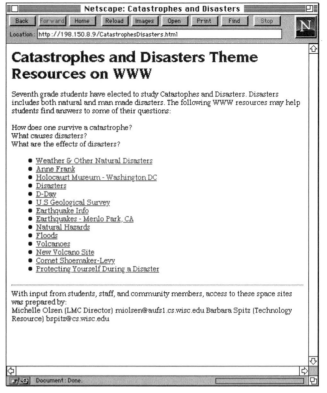

Figure 84: Example of a thematic site: a school curriculum.

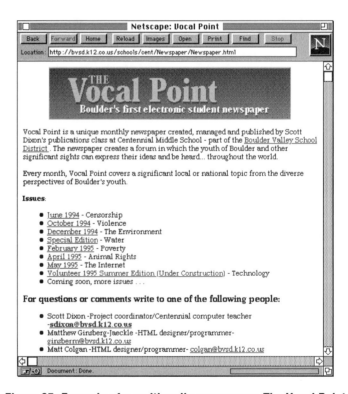

Figure 85: Example of a multimedia newspaper: *The Vocal Point* (http://bvsd.k12.co.us/schools/cent/Newspaper/Newspaper.html).

NOTES

1. For an excellent summary of HTML tags, see Kevin Werbach's *The Bare Bones Guide to HTML*. This short document is located on the WWW at http://www.access.digex.net/~werbach/barebone.html.

2. The program lynx (below left) is an example of a nongraphical WWW browser as opposed to a graphical browser like Netscape (below right).

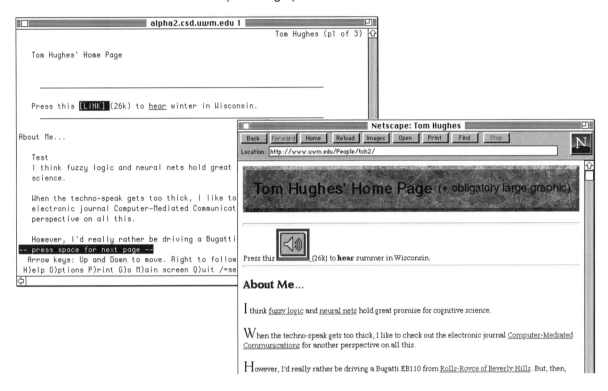

3. See E. Tittel, M. Gaither, S. Hassinger, and M. Erwin, *Foundations of World Wide Web programming with HTML and CGI*, (Foster City, CA: IDG Books Worldwide, 1995) for detailed information on the various HTML "flavors" and on advanced WWW programming.

4. According to *The 3rd WWW User Survey* conducted in 1995 by the Graphic, Visualization, and Usability Center (GVU) of the Georgia Institute of Technology, over half (55%) of the people surveyed said they learned HTML in only 1 to 3 hours. The GVU surveys are available at ftp.gvu.gatech.edu/pub/gvu/www/survey.

5. With a "shell" connection to the Internet, you can only view text. The WWW with all its graphics, etc., will not be accessible unless your Internet service provider offers SLIP or PPP access. Using one of these protocols, it's possible to get on the WWW.

6. A Macintosh file can be stored in two places: in a "data fork" and a "resource fork." Most of the time this need not concern you. However, it can be a problem when transferring Macintosh files to

other computers using ftp or other protocols. For example, Macintosh QuickTime movie files can be uploaded to the Internet and viewed by both Macintosh and Windows computers. But, before ftp'ing a QuickTime movie, the movie must go through a process called "flattening." The Movie Player application supplied with Macintosh's System 8 software can be used to flatten QuickTime movies.

7. J.G. Brooks and M.G. Brooks, *In search of understanding: The case for constructivist classrooms* (Alexandria, VA: ASCD, 1993) 17.

8. See B. G. Wilson, ed., *Constructivist Learning Environments* (Englewood Cliffs, NJ: Educational Technology Publications, 1996) for essays on computer-based microworlds.

APPENDIX A — ACCEPTABLE USE POLICY (AUP) SAMPLES

The following AUP examples are provided for reference purposes. Your own AUP must be based on your local situation and requirements.

For more information on AUPs, see the Internet site: gopher://riceinfo.rice.edu:1170/11/More/Acceptable.

Brevard County School District (Florida)

APPLICATION FOR ACCOUNT

AND

TERMS AND CONDITIONS FOR USE OF INTERNET

Please read the following carefully before signing this document. This is a legally binding document.

Internet access is now available to students and teachers in the Brevard County School District. The access is being offered as part of a collaborative research project involving Name Name High School (NNHS), Florida Institute of Technology, and the U.S. Department of Education. We are very pleased to bring this access to Brevard County and believe the Internet offers vast, diverse and unique resources to both students and teachers. Our goal in providing this service to teachers and students is to promote educational excellence in the Brevard County Schools by facilitating resource sharing, innovation and communication.

The Internet is an electronic highway connecting thousands of computers all over the world and millions of individual subscribers. Students and teachers have access to

1) electronic mail communication with people all over the world;
2) information and news from NASA as well as the opportunity to correspond with the scientists at NASA and other research institutions;
3) public domain and shareware of all types;
4) discussion groups on a plethora of topics ranging from Chinese culture to the environment to music to politics;
5) access to many University Library Catalogs, the Library of Congress, CARL and ERIC.

With access to computers and people all over the world also comes the availability of material that may not be considered to be of educational value in the context of the school setting. (NNHS), and Florida Institute of Technology have taken available precautions to restrict access to controversial materials. However, on a global network it is impossible to control all materials and an industrious user may discover controversial information. We ((NNHS), and Florida Institute of Technology) firmly believe that the valuable information and interaction available on this worldwide network far outweighs the possibility that users may procure material that is not consistent with the educational goals of this Project.

Internet access is coordinated through a complex association of government agencies, and regional and state networks. In addition, the smooth operation of the network relies upon the proper conduct of the end users who must adhere to strict guidelines. These guidelines are provided here so that you are aware of the responsibilities you are about to aquire. In general this requires efficient, ethical and legal utilization of the network resources. If a (NNHS) user violates any of these provisions, his or her account will be terminated and future access could possibly be denied. The signature(s) at the end of this document is (are) legally binding and indicates the party (parties) who signed has (have) read the terms and conditions carefully and understand(s) their significance.

Internet - Terms and Conditions

1) Acceptable Use - The purpose of NSFNET, which is the backbone network to the Internet, is to support research and education in and among academic institutions in the U.S. by providing access to unique resources and the opportunity for collaborative work. The use of your account must be in support of education and research and consistent with the educational objectives of the Brevard County School District. Use of other organization's network or computing resources must comply with the rules appropriate for that network. Transmission of any material in violation of any US or state regulation is prohibited. This includes, but is not limited to: copyrighted material, threatening or obscene material, or material protected by trade secret. Use for commercial activities by for-proFlorida Institute of Technology institutions is generally not acceptable. Use for product advertisement or political lobbying is also prohibited.

2) Privileges - The use of Internet is a privilege, not a right, and inappropriate use will result in a cancellation of those privileges. (Each student who receives an account will be part of a discussion with a (NNHS) faculty member pertaining to the proper use of the network.) The system administrators will deem what is inappropriate use and their decision is final. Also, the system administrators may close an account at any time as required. The administration, faculty, and staff of (NNHS) may request the system administrator to deny, revoke, or suspend specific user accounts.

3) Netiquette - You are expected to abide by the generally accepted rules of network etiquette. These include (but are not limited to) the following:
   a) Be polite. Do not get abusive in your messages to others.
   b) Use appropriate language. Do not swear, use vulgarities or any other inappropriate language. Illegal activities are strictly forbidden.
   c) Do not reveal your personal address or phone numbers of students or colleagues.
   d) Note that electronic mail (e-mail) is not guaranteed to be private. People who operate the system do have access to all

mail. Messages relating to or in support of illegal
activities may be reported to the authorities.
e) Do not use the network in such a way that you would
disrupt the use of the network by other users.
f) All communications and information accessible via the
network should be assumed to be private property.

4) (NNHS), and Florida Institute of Technology make no warranties of any
kind, whether expressed or implied, for the service it is providing.
(NNHS), and Florida Institute of Technology will not be responsible for any
damages you suffer. This include loss of data resulting from delays,
nondeliveries, misdeliveries, or service interruptions caused by it's own
negligence or your errors or omissions. Use of any information obtained
via (NNHS), or Florida Institute of Technology is at your own risk. (NNHS),
and Florida Institute of Technology specifically deny any responsibility
for the accuracy or quality of information obtained through its services.

5) Security - Security on any computer system is a high priority,
especially when the system involves many users. If you feel you can
identify a security problem on Internet, you must notify a system
administrator or e-mail barry@sci-ed.Florida Institute of Technology.edu.
Do not demonstrate the problem to other users. Do not use another
individual's account without written permission from that individual.
Attempts to login to Internet as a system administrator will result in
cancellation of user privileges. Any user identified as a security risk or
having a history of problems with other computer systems may be denied
access to Internet.

6) Vandalism - Vandalism will result in cancellation of privileges.
Vandalism is defined as any malicious attempt to harm or destroy data of
another user, Internet, or any of the above listed agencies or other
networks that are connected to the NSFNET Internet backbone. This
includes, but not limited to, the uploading or creation of computer
viruses.

7) Updating Your User Information - Internet may occasionally require new
registration and account information from you to continue the service. You
must notify Internet of any changes in your account information(address,
etc). Currently, there are no user fees for this service.

8) Exception of Terms and Condition - All terms and conditions as stated in
this document are applicable to the Brevard County School District, the
Florida Institute of Technology, in addition to NSFNET. These terms and
conditions reflect the entire agreement of the parties and supersedes all
prior oral or written agreements and understandings of the parties. These
terms and conditions shall be governed and interpreted in accordance with
the laws of the State of Florida, and the United States of America.

I understand and will abide by the above Terms and Conditions for Internet.
I further understand that any violation of the regulations above is

unethical and may constitute a criminal offense. Should I commit any
violation, my access privileges may be revoked, school disciplinary action
may be taken and/or appropriate legal action.

User Signature:_____ Date: ___/ ___/ ___
****
PARENT OR GUARDIAN (If you are under the age of 18 a parent or guardian
must also read and sign this agreement.)

As the parent or guardian of this student I have read the Terms and
Conditions for Internet access. I understand that this access is designed
for educational purposes and (NNHS), and Florida Institute of Technology
have taken available precautions to eliminate controversial material.
However, I also recognize it is impossible for (NNHS), and Florida
Institute of Technology to restrict access to all controversial materials
and I will not hold them responsible for materials acquired on the network.
Further, I accept full responsibility for supervision if and when my
child's use is not in a school setting. I hereby give permission to issue
an account for my child and certify that the information contained on this
form is correct.

Parent or Guardian (please print): _____

Signature: _____ Date: ___/ ___/ ___
****
SPONSORING TEACHER (Must be signed if the applicant is a student).
I have read the Terms and Conditions and agree to promote this agreement
with the student. Because the student may use the network for individual
work or in the context of another class, I cannot be held responsible for
the student use of the network. As the sponsoring teacher I do agree to
instruct the student on acceptable use of the network and proper network
etiquette.

Teacher's Name (please print): _____

Teacher's Signature: _____ Date: ___/ ___/ ___
****
APPLICATION PORTION OF DOCUMENT

User's Full Name (please print): _____

Home Address: _____

Home Phone: _____ Work Phone: _____

I am a.....
_____   (NNHS) student and will graduate in _____.

_____   (NNHS) teacher, teaching _____in grade_____ .

_____   (NNHS) staff working as a _____

_____   Brevard County School District community member.

When your account is established you will be notified of your logon name and user password. Thank you for your interest and support of this exciting new resource in the Brevard County Schools.

Poudre School District (Colorado)

Subject: Terms and Conditions of RMHSNet

RMHSNet - Terms and Conditions
(version 2.0, October 21, 1992)

GENERAL INFORMATION

Rocky Mountain High School Net (RMHSNet) is a service provided by
Rocky Mountain High School (RMHS) and the Poudre School District R-
1 (PR-1). Additional administrative support is provided by Colorado
State University (CSU) and CSUNET. The system administrators of
RMHSNet are employees of Poudre School District R-1 and reserve
the right to monitor all activity on RMHSNet. On acceptance for
membership to RMHSNet, members will be given an account name and
password. Although called a member "account", there are currently
no charges to members by RMHSNet for system usage.

RMHSNet is connected by a 56kbps dedicated link to CSUNET which in
turn is attached by a T1 (1.54 M) link to Colorado SuperNet, Inc.
(CSN) and their statewide backbone. A connection to the National
Science Foundation (NSF) NSFNET Internet backbone is made via the
University of Colorado to the National Center for Atmospheric
Research (NCAR) and also via Westnet in Utah.

Because of this complex association between so many government
agencies and networks, the end user of any of these networks must
adhere to strict guidelines. They are provided here so that members
and the parents of members who are under 18 years of age are aware
of the responsibilities they are about to acquire. RMHSNet may
modify these rules at any time by publishing the modified rule(s) on
the System. The signature(s) at the end of this document is (are)
legally binding and indicates the party (parties) who signed has
(have) read the terms and conditions carefully and understand their
significance.

INFORMATION CONTENT & USES OF THE SYSTEM

Member agrees not to publish on or over the System any information
which violates or infringes upon the rights of any other person or
any information which would be abusive, profane or sexually
offensive to an average person, or which, without the approval of the
system administrators, contains any advertising or any solicitation
of other members to use goods or services. Member agrees not to
use the facilities and capabilities of the System to conduct any
business or activity or solicit the performance of any activity which
is prohibited by law.

Because RMHSNet provides, through connection to Colorado SuperNet
and NSFNET, access to other computer systems around the world,

Member (and the parent(s) of Member if Member is under 18 years of age) specifically understands that the system administrators and Poudre R-1 do not have control of the content of information residing on these other systems. Members and the parents of members who are under 18 years of age are advised that some systems may contain defamatory, inaccurate, abusive, obscene, profane, sexually oriented, threatening, racially offensive, or illegal material. RMHSNet, Poudre School District R-1, and the system administrators do not condone the use of such materials and do not permit usage of such materials in the school environment. Parents of minors having accounts on the System should be aware of the existence of such materials and monitor home usage of the System. Students knowingly bringing such materials into the school environment will be dealt with according to the discipline policies of the individual school building and Poudre School District R-1, and such activities may result in termination of their account on RMHSNet.

RMHSNet, THE SYSTEM ADMINISTRATORS AND POUDRE SCHOOL DISTRICT R-1 DO NOT WARRANT THAT THE FUNCTIONS OR SERVICES PERFORMED BY, OR THAT THE INFORMATION OR SOFTWARE CONTAINED ON THE SYSTEM WILL MEET THE MEMBER'S REQUIREMENTS OR THAT THE OPERATION OF THE SYSTEM WILL BE UNINTERRUPTED OR ERROR-FREE OR THAT DEFECTS IN THE SYSTEM WILL BE CORRECTED. RMHSNet IS PROVIDED ON AN "AS IS, AS AVAILABLE" BASIS. RMHSNet DOES NOT MAKE ANY WARRANTIES, EXPRESS OR IMPLIED, INCLUDING, WITHOUT LIMITATION, THOSE OF MERCHANTABILITY AND FITNESS FOR A PARTICULAR PURPOSE, WITH RESPECT TO ANY SERVICES PROVIDED BY SAME AND ANY INFORMATION OR SOFTWARE CONTAINED THEREIN.

THIRD PARTY SUPPLIED INFORMATION

Opinions, advice, services and all other information expressed by members, information providers, service providers, or other third party personnel on RMHSNet are those of the provider and not of RMHSNet. Members are urged to seek professional advice for specific, individual situations.

Member may order services or merchandise from other agencies and members of RMHSNet, not affiliated with RMHSNet, ("Seller") through RMHSNet. All matters concerning the merchandise and services ordered from Seller, including but not limited to purchase terms, payment terms, warranties, guarantees, maintenance and delivery, are solely between the Seller and the Member. RMHSNet makes no warranties or representations whatsoever with regard to any goods or services provided by Sellers. RMHSNet, Poudre School District R-1, or the system administrators shall not be a party to such transactions or be liable for any costs or damages arising out of, either directly or indirectly, the actions or inactions of Sellers.

TELEPHONE CHARGES

RMHSNet assumes no responsibility or liability for any phone charges including, but not limited to, long distance charges, per minute (unit) surcharges and/or equipment or line costs, incurred by Member while accessing RMHSNet. Any disputes or problems regarding phone service are strictly between Member and his or her local phone company and/or long distance service provider.

UPDATING MEMBER ACCOUNT INFORMATION

RMHSNet may occasionally require new registration and account information from members to continue the service. Member must notify RMHSNet of any changes in account information (address, phone, name, etc.).

ONLINE CONDUCT

Any action by a member that is determined by a system administrator to constitute an inappropriate use of RMHSNet or to improperly restrict or inhibit other members from using and enjoying RMHSNet is strictly prohibited and may result in termination of an offending member's account. Member specifically agrees not to submit, publish, or display on RMHSNet any defamatory, inaccurate, abusive, obscene, profane, sexually oriented, threatening, racially offensive, or illegal material; nor shall Member encourage the use of controlled substances. Transmission of material, information or software in violation of any local, state or federal law is prohibited and is a breach of the Terms and Conditions.

Member specifically agrees to indemnify RMHSNet, Poudre School District R-1, and the system administrators for any losses, costs, or damages, including reasonable attorneys' fees incurred by RMHSNet, Poudre School District R-1, and the system administrators relating to, or arising out of any breach of this section (Online Conduct) by Member.

RMHSNet is to be used by Member for his/her personal use only. Commercial uses of RMHSNet are strictly prohibited unless prior written consent from the system administrators has been granted.

SOFTWARE LIBRARIES: Only public domain files, and files in which the author has given expressed consent for online distribution, may be uploaded to the software libraries by Member. Any other software may not be uploaded to the software libraries. Any software having the purpose of damaging other members' systems, or the RMHSNET System (e.g., computer viruses) is specifically prohibited. The system administrators, at their sole discretion, reserve the right to refuse posting of files, and to remove files. The system administrators, at their sole discretion, further reserve the right to immediately terminate the account of a member who misuses the software libraries. System administrators do not necessarily inspect software uploaded by members and RMHSNet does not guarantee the suitability or performance of any software downloaded from RMHSNet System or any other system accessed through RMHSNet.

COPYRIGHTED MATERIAL: Copyrighted material must not be placed on any system connected to RMHSNet without the author's permission. Only the owner(s) or persons they specifically authorize may upload copyrighted material to the Service. Members may download copyrighted material for their own use. Any member may also non-commercially redistribute a copyrighted program with the expressed permission of the owner or authorized person. Permission must be specified in the document, on the System, or must be obtained directly from the author.

PUBLIC DOMAIN MATERIAL: Any member may upload public domain programs to the System. Any member may download public domain programs for their own use or non-commercially redistribute a public domain program. Member assumes all risks regarding the determination of whether a program is in the public domain.

PUBLIC POSTING AREAS (MESSAGE BOARDS/USENET GROUPS): UseNet messages are posted from systems connected to NSFNet around the world and the RMHSNet system administrators have no control on the content of messages posted from these other systems. To best utilize system resources, the system administrators will determine which UseNet groups are most applicable to the curricular needs of the school district and will carry these groups on the local system. The system administrators, at their sole discretion, may remove messages posted locally that are deemed to be unacceptable or in violation of the Terms and Conditions. The system administrators, at their sole discretion, further reserve the right to immediately terminate the account of a member who misuses the message boards or UseNet groups.

REAL-TIME/INTERACTIVE COMMUNICATIONS AREAS: The system administrators, at their sole discretion, reserve the right to immediately terminate the account of a member who misuses the real-time conference features (talk/chat/internet relay chat).

ELECTRONIC MAIL: Electronic mail ("Mail") is a private electronic message sent by or to a member in correspondence with another person having Internet mail access. Messages received by the System are retained on the System until deleted by the recipient. A canceled RMHSNet account will not retain its Mail. Members are expected to remove old messages in a timely fashion and the system administrators may remove such messages if not attended to regularly by the member. The system administrators will not intentionally inspect the contents of Mail sent by one member to an identified addressee, or disclose such contents to other than the sender, or an intended recipient, without the consent of the sender or an intended recipient, unless required to do so by law or policies of Poudre School District R-1, or to investigate complaints regarding Mail which is alleged to contain defamatory, inaccurate, abusive, obscene, profane, sexually oriented, threatening, racially offensive, or illegal material. RMHSNet reserves the right to cooperate fully with Poudre School District R-1, local, state, or federal officials in any investigation concerning or relating to any Mail transmitted on RMHSNet.

DISK USAGE: The system administrators reserve the right to set quotas for disk usage on the System. A member who exceeds their quota will be advised to delete files to return to compliance. Members may request that their disk quota be increased by submitting a request via electronic mail to help@lobo.rmh.pr1.k12.co.us stating the need for the quota increase. A member who remains in non-compliance of disk space quotas after seven (7) days of notification will have their files removed by a system administrator.

SECURITY: Security on any computer system is a high priority, especially when the system involves many users. If a member feels that they can identify a security problem on RMHSNet, the member must notify a system administrator or e-mail help@lobo.rmh.pr1.k12.co.us. The member should not demonstrate the problem to others. A Poudre R-1 staff person may allow students who are not members to access the system through the staff person's account as long as the staff person does not disclose the password of the account to the students and understands that the staff person assumes responsibility for the actions of students using their account. Members may not otherwise let others use their account and password. Passwords to the system should not be easily guessable by others, nor should they be words which could be found in a dictionary. Attempts to login to the system using another member's account or as a system administrator will result in termination of the account. Member should immediately notify a system administrator (help@lobo.rmh.pr1.k12.co.us) if their password is lost or stolen, or if they have reason to believe that someone has obtained unauthorized access to their account. Any member identified as a security risk or having a history of problems with other computer systems may be denied access to RMHSNet.

VANDALISM: Vandalism will result in cancellation of privileges. Vandalism is defined as any malicious attempt to harm or destroy data of another member, RMHSNet, or any of the agencies or other networks that are connected to CSUNET, CSN, or the NSFNET Internet backbone. This includes, but is not limited to, the uploading or creation of computer viruses.

TERMINATION OF ACCOUNT

A member's access to, and use of, RMHSNet may be terminated by the member sending Notice to a system administrator. Terminations by Member will be effective on the day that a system administrator receives Notice or on a future date if so specified in the Notice. Accounts which are inactive for more than 30 days may be removed along with that member's files without Notice given to the member.

The system administrators reserve the right, at their sole discretion, to suspend or terminate Member's access to and use of RMHSNet upon any breach of the Terms and Conditions by Member. Prior to a suspension or termination, or as soon after as is practicable, the system administrator will inform the member of the suspected breach and give the member an opportunity to present an explanation. Member may request a review hearing with a different system administrator than the system administrator who imposed the suspension or termination within seven (7) days of such suspension or termination if Member feels that such action was unjust. After the review, access may be restored if the system administrator upholds Member's appeal.

OTHER PROVISIONS

The Terms and Conditions shall be interpreted, construed and enforced in all respects in accordance with the laws of the State of Colorado. Each party irrevocably consents to the jurisdiction of the courts of the State of Colorado and the federal courts situated in the State of Colorado, in connection with any action to enforce the provisions of the Terms and Conditions, to recover damages or other relief for breach or default under the Terms and Conditions, or otherwise arising under or by reason of the Terms and Conditions.

EXCEPTION OF TERMS AND CONDITIONS

All terms and conditions of Colorado SuperNet, Inc. and NSFNET, as stated in the following paragraphs are also applicable. They are printed below for your review.

Colorado SuperNet, Inc. Terms and Conditions
(version 1.0, December 27, 1990)

1.   Colorado SuperNet, Inc. (CSN) may only be used for lawful purposes. Transmission of any material in violation of any US or state regulation is prohibited. This includes, but is not limited to: copyrighted material, threatening or obscene material, or material protected by trade secret. You agree to indemnify and hold harmless CSN from any claims resulting from your use of the service which

damages you or another party.

2.   Use of any information obtained via CSN is at your own risk.
CSN specifically denies any responsibility for the accuracy or
quality of information obtained through its services. CSN exercises
no control whatsoever over the content of the information residing
on or passing through it. This account is not to facilitate access to
commercial, for-pay services.

3.   CSN makes no warranties of any kind, whether expressed or
implied, for the service it is providing. CSN also disclaims any
warranty of merchantability or fitness for a particular purpose. CSN
will not be responsible for any damages you suffer. This includes
loss of data resulting from delays, non-deliveries, misdeliveries, or
service interruptions caused by it's own negligence or your errors or
omissions.

4.   Use of other organization's networks or computing resources
must comply with the rules appropriate for that network. You agree
to abide by the Interim NSFNET Appropriate Use Policy, as
applicable.

Interim NSFNET Acceptable Use Policy

The purpose of NSFNET is to support research and education in and
among academic institutions in the U.S. by providing access to
unique resources and the opportunity for collaborative work. This
statement represents a guide to the acceptable use of the Internet
backbone. It is expected that the various middle level networks will
formulate their own use policies for traffic that will not traverse
the backbone.

1.   All use must be consistent with the purposes of NSFNET.

2.   The intent of the use policy is to make clear certain cases
which are consistent with the purposes of NSFNET, not to
exhaustively enumerate all such possible uses.

3.   The NSF NSFNET Project Office may at any time make
determination that particular uses are or are not consistent with
the purposes of NSFNET. Such determinations will be reported to the
NSFNET Policy Advisory Committee and to the user community.

4.   If a use is consistent with the purposes of NSFNET, then
activities in direct support of that use will be considered consistent
with the purposes of NSFNET. For example, administrative
communications for the support infrastructure needed for research
and instruction are acceptable.

5.   Use in support of research or instruction at not-for-profit
institutions of research or instruction in the United States is
acceptable.

6.   Use for a project which is part of or supports a research or
instruction activity for a not-for-profit institution of research or
instruction in the United States is acceptable, even if any or all
parties to the use are located or employed elsewhere. For example,
communications directly between industrial affiliates engaged in
support of a project for such an institution is acceptable.

7.   Use for commercial activities by for-profit institutions is
generally not acceptable unless it can be justified under (4) above.
These should be reviewed on a case-by-case basis by the NSF
Project Office.

8.   Use for research or instruction at for-profit institutions may
or may not be consistent with the purposes of NSFNET, and will be
reviewed by the NSF Projects Office on a case-by-case basis.

Member Signature (as it appears on the application)   Date

Parent Signature (if Member is under 18 years of age)   Date

System Administrator   Date

This Terms and Conditions agreement must be returned to Sarah
Brennan at the Poudre School District R-1 Media Center prior to
opening a member account.   A copy should be retained by the member/parent.

APPENDIX B — INTERNET SITES OF INTEREST TO EDUCATORS

Newsgroups

- *k12.chat.elementary*—casual conversation for elementary students, grades K-5.
- *k12.chat.junior*—casual conversation for students in grades 6-8.
- *k12.chat.senior*—casual conversation for high school students.
- *k12.chat.teacher*—casual conversation for teachers grades K-12.
- *k12.ed.art*—arts and craft curricula in K-12 education.
- *k12.ed.business*—business educational curricula in grades K-12.
- *k12.ed.comp.literacy*—teaching computer literacy in grades K-12.
- *k12.ed.healthpe*—health and physical education curricula in grades K-12.
- *k12.ed.lifeskills*—home economics, career education, and school counseling.
- *k12.ed.math*—mathematics curriculum in K-12 education.
- *k12.ed.music*—music education and performing arts curriculum in grades K-12.
- *k12.ed.science*—science curriculum for grades K-12.
- *k12.ed.socstudies*—geography, civics, political science, and history curriculum for K-12.
- *k12.ed.special*—education of students with special needs.
- *k12.ed.tag*—K-12 curriculum for gifted and talented students.
- *k12.ed.tech*—industrial arts and vocational education.
- *k12.lang.art*—language arts (reading, writing, literature) instruction.
- *k12.lang.deutscheng*—bilingual German/English practice with native speakers.
- *k12.lang.espeng*—bilingual Spanish/English practice with native speakers.
- *k12.lang.francais*—French practice with native speakers.
- *k12.lang.russian*—bilingual Russian/English practice with native speakers.
- *k12.library*—implementing information technology in school libraries.
- *k12.sys.ch0*—(through ch12) current projects.
- *k12.sys.projects*—potential projects.

Listservs

AAASEST	AAASEST@GWUVM.GWU.EDU	Perspectives on Ethical Issues in Science and Technology
AAASHRAN	AAASHRAN@GWUVM.GWU.EDU	AAAS Human Rights Action Network
AATG	AATG@INDYCMS.IUPUI.EDU	American Association of Teachers of German
ACADV	ACADV@VM1.NODAK.EDU	ACADV Academic Advising Forum
ADD-L	ADD-L@ADMIN.HUMBERC.ON.CA	Forum for discussion of concerns of drinking and driving
AE	AE@SJSUVM1.SJSU.EDU	Alternative Energy Discussion List
AECP-L	AECP-L@UNBVM1.CSD.UNB.CA	Apple Education Consultants Program
AEE	AEE@MIAMIU.MUOHIO.EDU	Alternative Educational Environments
AEELIST	AEELIST@PUCC.PRINCETON.EDU	Association for Experiential Education
AEMA-L	AEMA-L@ASUVM.INRE.ASU.EDU	AEMA-L: Arizona Educational Media Association
AERA-A	AERA-A@ASUVM.INRE.ASU.EDU	AERA-A Division A: Educational Administration Forum
AERA-B	AERA-B@ASUVM.INRE.ASU.EDU	AERA-B Division B: Curriculum Studies Forum
AERA-C	AERA-C@ASUVM.INRE.ASU.EDU	AERA-C Division C: Learning and Instruction
AERA-D	AERA-D@ASUVM.INRE.ASU.EDU	AERA-D Division D: Measurement and Research Methodology
AERA-E	AERA-E@ASUVM.INRE.ASU.EDU	AERA-E Division E: Counseling and Human Development
AERA-F	AERA-F@ASUVM.INRE.ASU.EDU	AERA-F Division F: History and Historiography
AERA-G	AERA-G@ASUVM.INRE.ASU.EDU	AERA-G Division G: Social Context of Education
AERA-GSL	AERA-GSL@ASUVM.INRE.ASU.EDU	Graduate Studies Discussion Forum
AERA-H	AERA-H@ASUVM.INRE.ASU.EDU	AERA-H Division H: School Evaluation and Program Development
AERA-I	AERA-I@ASUVM.INRE.ASU.EDU	AERA-I Division I: Education in the Professions
AERA-J	AERA-J@ASUVM.INRE.ASU.EDU	AERA-J Division J: Postsecondary Education
AERA-K	AERA-K@ASUVM.INRE.ASU.EDU	AERA-K Division K: Teaching and Teacher Education

AERA-TC	AERA-TC@UNBVM1.CSD.UNB.CA	AERA Ad Hoc Committee on Telecommunications
AERA-VC	AERA-VC@UNBVM1.CSD.UNB.CA	VirtCon: AERA's Virtual Conference (ENET SIG)
AFROAM-L	AFROAM-L@HARVARDA.BITNET	Critical Issues in African American Life and Culture
ALTLEARN	ALTLEARN@SJUVM.STJOHNS.EDU	Alternative Approaches to Learning Discussion List
ANI-L	ANI-L@UTKVM1.UTK.EDU	Autism Network International
APPL-L	APPL-L@VM.CC.UNI.TORUN.PL	Computer applications in science and education
ARTCRIT	ARTCRIT@VM1.YORKU.CA	Art Criticism Discussion Forum
ASCD-SCI	ASCD-SCI@PSUVM.PSU.EDU	Alliance for Teaching of Science
ASPIRE-L	ASPIRE-L@IUBVM.UCS.INDIANA.EDU	ASPIRE-L: Linkages for Students from Asian Nations
ASTA-L	ASTA-L@CMSUVMB.BITNET	American String Teachers Association List
ATHTRN-L	ATHTRN-L@IUBVM.UCS.INDIANA.EDU	Discussion list for athletic trainers
AUSTEN-L	AUSTEN-L@VM1.MCGILL.CA	Jane Austen discussion list
AUTISM	AUTISM@SJUVM.STJOHNS.EDU	SJU Autism and Developmental Disabilities List
AUTOCAT	AUTOCAT@UBVM.CC.BUFFALO.EDU	AUTOCAT: Library cataloging and authorities discussion group
AZTLAN	AZTLAN@ULKYVM.LOUISVILLE.EDU	Pre-Columbian History
BATECH-L	BATECH-L@PSUVM.PSU.EDU	Technologies in Business Education
BIOCIS-L	BIOCIS-L@SIVM.SI.EDU	Biology Curriculum Innovation Study
BIODIDAC	BIODIDAC@ACADVM1.UOTTAWA.CA	Electronic Discussion Group for Biology teachers
BIOPI-L	BIOPI-L@KSUVM.KSU.EDU	Secondary Biology Teacher Enhancement PI
BIOSPH-L	BIOSPH-L@UBVM.CC.BUFFALO.EDU	Biosphere, ecology discussion list
BUGNET	BUGNET@WSUVM1.CSC.WSU.EDU	Insect Education
BUSED-L	BUSED-L@MAX.CC.UREGINA.CA	A Forum for Discussion of Business Education Teaching Practices
CALIBK12	CALIBK12@SJSUVM1.SJSU.EDU	California K-12 Librarians
CAOM	CAOM@SJSUVM1.SJSU.EDU	California Odyssey of the Mind
CAP-L	CAP-L@VM1.SPCS.UMN.EDU	Discussion of Contemporary American Poetry
CESNEWS	CESNEWS@BROWNVM.BROWN.EDU	Coalition of Essential Schools News

CEUT-L	CEUT-L@VTVM1.CC.VT.EDU	Dialogue for Teaching and Learning Issues
CHICLE	CHICLE@UNMVMA.UNM.EDU	Chicano literature discussion list
CHILDLIT	CHILDLIT@RUTVM1.RUTGERS.EDU	Children's Literature: Criticism and Theory
CHLD+FAM	CHLD+FAM@SUVM.SYR.EDU	Academic discussion of topics in Child and Family Studies
COMMED	COMMED@VM.ITS.RPI.EDU	Communication education
CPSI-L	CPSI-L@UBVM.CC.BUFFALO.EDU	Creative Problem Solving Institute list
CSEA-L	CSEA-L@UNBVM1.CSD.UNB.CA	Canadian Society for Education Through Art
CULTUR-L	CULTUR-L@VM.TEMPLE.EDU	Cultural differences in curriculum discussion
CURDEV-L	CURDEV-L@PSUORVM.CC.PDX.EDU	Science Curriculum Development List
CURRENT	CURRENT@UMSLVMA.UMSL.EDU	Campus Newspaper Discussion List
CURRICUL	CURRICUL@VM.CC.PURDUE.EDU	CPT Curriculum Mailing List
CUR343-L	CUR343-L@QUCDN.QUEENSU.CA	A B.Ed. Course: Secondary School Mathematics
CUSEN-L	CUSEN-L@QUCDN.QUEENSU.CA	Canadian Unified Student Environmental Network
CX-L	CX-L@UGA.CC.UGA.EDU	Discussion High School Debate
DEAFKIDS	DEAFKIDS@SJUVM.STJOHNS.EDU	DeafKids List for Deaf Children
DEOS-L	DEOS-L@PSUVM.PSU.EDU	DEOS-L - The Distance Education Online Symposium
DICKNS-L	DICKNS-L@UCSBVM.UCSB.EDU	Charles Dickens Forum
DRUGABUS	DRUGABUS@UMAB.BITNET	Drug Abuse Education Information and Research
DRUGHIED	DRUGHIED@TAMVM1.TAMU.EDU	Drug Abatement Research Discussion
ECENET-L	ECENET-L@VMD.CSO.UIUC.EDU	Early childhood education/young children (0-8)
ECEOL-L	ECEOL-L@MAINE.MAINE.EDU	Early Childhood Education online mailing list
EDLAW	EDLAW@UKCC.UKY.EDU	Law and Education
EDNETNY	EDNETNY@SUVM.SYR.EDU	Educational Development Network of New York
EDNEWS	EDNEWS@VM.CC.PURDUE.EDU	News Service Education News releases
EDPOLYAN	EDPOLYAN@ASUVM.INRE.ASU.EDU	Education Policy Analysis Forum

EDPOLYAR	EDPOLYAR@ASUVM.INRE.ASU.EDU	EDUC POLICY ANALYSIS ARCHIVES: An Electronic Journal
EDP513	EDP513@LISTSERV.ARIZONA.EDU	Research in Educational Technologies
EDREF-L	EDREF-L@ADMIN.HUMBERC.ON.CA	Educational Reform Discussion Group
EDRES-DB	EDRES-DB@UNBVM1.CSD.UNB.CA	Educational Resources on the Internet - Database
EDRES-L	EDRES-L@UNBVM1.CSD.UNB.CA	Educational Resources on the Internet
EDST-L	EDST-L@VM.CC.PURDUE.EDU	Educational Studies Faculty and Staff - List
EDSTART	EDSTART@UNBVM1.CSD.UNB.CA	Ed Students Announcements, Ramblings & Twaddle
EDSTYLE	EDSTYLE@SJUVM.STJOHNS.EDU	The Learning Styles Theory and Research List
EDTECH	EDTECH@MSU.EDU	EDTECH - Educational Technology
EDTECH-L	EDTECH-L@UKANVM.CC.UKANS.EDU	A list for the education technology committee
EDTECPOL	EDTECPOL@UMDD.BITNET	Conference on Educational Technology Policy
EDTEL505	EDTEL505@INDYCMS.IUPUI.EDU	Educational Telecommunications R 505
EDUCATIONAL-R	ERL-L@ASUVM.INRE.ASU.EDU	Educational Research List (ASUACAD)
EDUCOM-W	EDUCOM-W@BITNIC.EDUCOM.EDU	EDUCOM-W - EDUCOM Women and Information Technology List
EDUEXC-L	EDUEXC-L@ASUVM.INRE.ASU.EDU	Educational Excellence Information Exchange
EDULAC	EDULAC@ENLACE.BITNET	EDULAC: Educadores Latinoamericanos en Ciencias de la Informa+
EDUMATE	EDUMATE@USACHVM1.BITNET	Educacion Matematica en Chile
EDUTEL	EDUTEL@VM.ITS.RPI.EDU	Education and information technologies
EEACT-L	EEACT-L@QUCDN.QUEENSU.CA	Eastern Ontario Environmental Education Action Network
ENGLED-L	ENGLED-L@PSUVM.PSU.EDU	English Education
EST-L	EST-L@ASUVM.INRE.ASU.EDU	Teachers of English for Science and Technology
FLAC-L	FLAC-L@BROWNVM.BROWN.EDU	Foreign Language Across Curriculum List

GEOED-L	GEOED-L@UWF.CC.UWF.EDU	Geology and Earth Science Education Discussion Forum
GEOGED	GEOGED@UKCC.UKY.EDU	Geography Education List
GLBL-HS	GLBL-HS@OCMVM.CNYRIC.ORG	Global Studies High School
H-CIVWAR	H-CIVWAR@UICVM.UIC.EDU	H-Net US Civil War History discussion list
H-HIGH-S	H-HIGH-S@MSU.EDU	An H-Net List for Teaching Social Studies in Secondary Schools
H-POL	H-POL@KSUVM.KSU.EDU	H-Net Political History discussion list
H-TEACH	H-TEACH@UICVM.UIC.EDU	H-Net List for Teaching History and Related Fields
HOLMESGP	HOLMESGP@MSU.EDU	HOLMES ED School Reform
HPSST-L	HPSST-L@QUCDN.QUEENSU.CA	History and Philosophy of Science and Science Teaching
HSJOURN	HSJOURN@VM.CC.LATECH.EDU	High School Scholastic Journalism
IMSE-L	IMSE-L@UICVM.UIC.EDU	Institute for Math and Science Education
INTER-ED	INTER-ED@VM1.SPCS.UMN.EDU	Forum for People with Interest in International Education
I3ECON	I3ECON@CCVM.SUNYSB.EDU	Innovation in Instruction of Economics
JCMST-L	JCMST-L@VM.CC.PURDUE.EDU	JOURNAL OF COMPUTERS IN MATHEMATICS AND SCIENCE TEACHING
JEI-L	JEI-L@UMDD.BITNET	Technology in Education Mailing List
JOURNET	JOURNET@QUCDN.QUEENSU.CA	Discussion List for Journalism Education
JTE-L	JTE-L@VTVM1.CC.VT.EDU	Journal of Technology Education electronic journal
K-16LINK	K-16LINK@UGA.CC.UGA.EDU	Technology and Writing, K-16
KIDCAFE	KIDCAFE@VM1.NODAK.EDU	KIDCAFE Youth Dialog
KIDCAFEJ	KIDCAFEJ@VM1.NODAK.EDU	Japanese Youth Dialog
KIDCAFEN	KIDCAFEN@VM1.NODAK.EDU	KIDCAFEN Scandinavian Dialog
KIDCAFEP	KIDCAFEP@VM1.NODAK.EDU	Portuguese Youth Dialog
KIDCAFES	KIDCAFES@VM1.NODAK.EDU	KIDCAFES Spanish Dialog
KIDFORUM	KIDFORUM@VM1.NODAK.EDU	KIDFORUM KIDLink Coordination
KIDINTRO	KIDINTRO@SJUVM.STJOHNS.EDU	Site introducing Children to Project Chatback
KIDLEADJ	KIDLEADJ@VM1.NODAK.EDU	Japanese KIDLink Coordination
KIDLEADN	KIDLEADN@VM1.NODAK.EDU	Scandinavian KIDLink Coordination

KIDLEADP	KIDLEADP@VM1.NODAK.EDU	Portuguese KIDLink Coordination
KIDLEADR	KIDLEADR@VM1.NODAK.EDU	KIDLEADR KIDLink Coordination
KIDLEADS	KIDLEADS@VM1.NODAK.EDU	Spanish KIDLink Coordination
KIDLINK	KIDLINK@VM1.NODAK.EDU	KIDLINK Project List
KIDLIT-L	KIDLIT-L@BINGVMB.CC.BINGHAMTON.EDU	Children and Youth Literature List
KIDNEWS	KIDNEWS@VM1.NODAK.EDU	KIDLink Newsletter Distribution
KIDPLAN	KIDPLAN@VM1.NODAK.EDU	KIDPLAN KIDLink Planning
KIDPLAN2	KIDPLAN2@VM1.NODAK.EDU	KIDPLAN2 Kidlink Work Group
KIDPROJ	KIDPROJ@VM1.NODAK.EDU	Special KIDLink Projects
KIDS-ACT	KIDS-ACT@VM1.NODAK.EDU	KIDS-ACT What can I do now?
KIDZMAIL	KIDZMAIL@ASUVM.INRE.ASU.EDU	KIDZMAIL: Kids exploring issues and interests electronically
K12ADMIN	K12ADMIN@SUVM.SYR.EDU	K-12 Educators Interested in Educational Administration
K12PALS	K12PALS@SUVM.SYR.EDU	List for teachers to help students seeking penpals
K12STCTE	K12STCTE@BITNIC.EDUCOM.EDU	Consortium for School Networking (CoSN) Officers, Board Member+
LEADTCHR	LEADTCHR@PSUVM.PSU.EDU	Networking lead teachers
MEDIA-L	MEDIA-L@BINGVMB.CC.BINGHAMTON.EDU	Media in Education
MIDDLE-L	MIDDLE-L@VMD.CSO.UIUC.EDU	Middle level education/early adolescence (10-14)
MULTI-L	MULTI-L@VM.BIU.AC.IL	Language and Education in Multi-Lingual Settings
MUSIC-ED	MUSIC-ED@VM1.SPCS.UMN.EDU	MUSIC-ED Music Education
NAEATASK	NAEATASK@LISTSERV.ARIZONA.EDU	NAEA Art Teacher Education Task Force
NCPRSE-L	NCPRSE-L@ECUVM.CIS.ECU.EDU	Reform discussion list for Science Education
NETSEARCH	NETSRCH@IUBVM.UCS.INDIANA.EDU	Workshops for Grades K-12: Internet Searching for Educators
NETSERVER	NETSERV@IUBVM.UCS.INDIANA.EDU	Workshops for Grades K-12: Creating Internet Servers
NMCTE	NMCTE@UNMVMA.UNM.EDU	New Mexico Council on Technology in Education
NSLCK-12	NSLCK-12@VM1.SPCS.UMN.EDU	K-12 Service-Learning Nationwide
OSF-EDUC	OSF-EDUC@IB.RL.AC.UK	Open Software Foundation, Educational Mailing List
PENPAL	PENPAL©L@UNCCUM.BITNET	Assistance in locating e-mail penpals for schools

PHYS-L	PHYS-L@UWF.CC.UWF.EDU	Forum for Physics Teachers
PHYSHARE	PHYSHARE@PSUVM.PSU.EDU	Sharing resources for high school physics
PSATC-L	PSATC-L@UBVM.CC.BUFFALO.EDU	Problem Solving Across the Curriculum List
RIP-EXP	RIP-EXP@BROWNVM.BROWN.EDU	Rhode Island K-12 experiences
RIP-FUND	RIP-FUND@BROWNVM.BROWN.EDU	Rhode Island K-12 providers, funding
RIP-INFO	RIP-INFO@BROWNVM.BROWN.EDU	Rhode Island K-12 information
RIP-SS	RIP-SS@BROWNVM.BROWN.EDU	Rhode Island K-12 social studies
RIP-STAF	RIP-STAF@BROWNVM.BROWN.EDU	Rhode Island K-12 providers, staff
RIP-TECH	RIP-TECH@BROWNVM.BROWN.EDU	Rhode Island K-12 providers, technology
T-AMLIT	T-AMLIT@BITNIC.EDUCOM.EDU	Teaching the American Literatures
TEACHING	TEACHING@VM1.MCGILL.CA	Teaching discussion group
TEACHMAT	TEACHMAT@UICVM.UIC.EDU	Methods of Teaching Mathematics
TEACHNET	TEACHNET@KENTVM.KENT.EDU	Teachers and Student Discussions
TESL-L	TESL-L@CUNYVM.CUNY.EDU	TESL-L: Teachers of English as a Second Language List
T321-L	T321-L@MIZZOU1.MISSOURI.EDU	Teaching Science in Elementary Schools
UAARTED	UAARTED@LISTSERV.ARIZONA.EDU	Art Education Issues
VT-HSNET	VT-HSNET@VTVM1.CC.VT.EDU	Vermont K-12 School Network
VTBIOTEC	VTBIOTEC@VTVM1.CC.VT.EDU	K–14 biotech education

APPENDIX C — INTERNET SERVICE PROVIDERS AND ISDN INFORMATION

National service providers

Note: These providers may not have Internet service available in your area. Contact the provider for further information.

- America Online
  800-827-6364

- Concentric Research Corporation
  400 41st Street
  Bay City, MI 48708
  800-745-2747

- Delphi Internet Services Corporation
  1030 Massachusetts Avenue
  Cambridge, MA 02138
  800-695-4005

- Global Connect, Inc.
  497 Queens Creek Road
  Williamsburg, VA 23185
  804-229-4484

- Information Access Technologies, Inc. (Holonet)
  46 Shattuck Square
  Suite 11
  Berkeley, CA 94704
  510-704-0160

- Moran Communications
  1576 Sweet Home Road
  Amherst, NY 14228
  716-639-1254

- Performance Systems International
  510 Huntmar Park Drive
  Herndon, VA 22070
  800-827-7482

- Portal Information Network
  20863 Stevens Creek Blvd.
  Suite 200
  Cupertino, CA 95014
  408-973-9111

- Prodigy
  800-PRODIGY

- SprintLink
  12502 Sunrise Valley Dr.
  Reston, VA 22096
  703-827-7240 or 800-817-7755

ISDN information

Because an ISDN connection to the Internet requires installation of a special phone line to your home or school, your local phone company is a good place to start asking questions.

If you already have WWW access, "Dan Kegel's Home Page" (http://www.alumni.caltech.edu/~dank/isdn/) is a great source of ISDN information.

- National ISDN Hotline
  800-992-ISDN
  201-829-2263 (Fax)
  isdn@cc.bellcore.com (e-mail)
  http://www.bellcore.com (WWW)

- Ameritech
  800-832-6328
  http://www.aads.net

- Bell Atlantic
  800-570-ISDN
  http://www.ba.com

- Bell South
  800-858-9413
  http://www.bst.bls.com

- NYNEX
  800-GET-ISDN

- Pacific Bell
  800-472-ISDN
  http://www.pacbell.com

- Southwestern Bell
  800-992-ISDN
  http://www.sbc.com

- U. S. West
  303-965-7073

APPENDIX D — CHECKLIST FOR EVALUATING INTERNET INFORMATION

Purpose and audience

Consider the intent of this information and why it is being communicated.

☐ Is this material designed for your student audience?

☐ What is the goal of the site?

☐ Who supports this site and what is their goal in presenting this information?

Authority

Consider the credentials of the individual(s) or groups presenting this information. If not provided, send them an e-mail message and request information on their credentials.

☐ Does the individual or group who constructed this information have the knowledge or experience to be considered reliable?

☐ Does the author cite other authorities?

☐ Are you confident that the individual or group that constructed this information is well qualified?

Scope

Consider the breadth and detail of the information provided.

☐ Skim the headings, table of contents, pictorial/graphic information. Does the content appear to be useful for your purpose?

☐ Does this site provide links to other sites that would allow for greater breadth or detail? Do you need to conduct a search to find additional information?

Format

Consider how the information is presented, how easily it can be interpreted, and whether it can be readily acquired or reproduced.

☐ Is the material clearly presented? Look for a table of contents, index, or preview that describes the site's content.

☐ Is the information presented in a format that is easily understood?

☐ Is there a statement as to whether you can reproduce this information for educational purposes?

Acceptance of material

Consider the opinion others have of this material.

☐ Have you contacted others on the Net to determine if the material is useful?

☐ Does this material come from a source that is widely recognized?

☐ Does the site provide information as to how many individuals access the site?

Suggestions for classroom use

Acquaint students with these criteria by providing them examples of materials selected from the Internet that display the qualities addressed in the criteria. We would suggest that a range of materials be used. That is, display examples of material that is widely accepted and material that is likely to be used by a small group of individuals.

Once students have acquired a basic understanding of the checklist, you may consider selecting material, then posting a message on a student discussion group such as k12.chat.elementary (grades K-5), k12.chat.junior (grades 6-8), or k12.chat.senior (high school) requesting others to examine that material and evaluate it using the criteria above.

GLOSSARY

AUP	(Acceptable Use Policy) This is an agreement generally drawn up for school districts that defines the rules and behaviors of students when they are connected to the Internet. These policies address such issues as the use of abusive language, engaging in illegal acts on the Internet, and accessing inappropriate information.
baud rate	A unit of measurement to indicate how much information in bits is being transmitted. Normally baud rates are expressed in bits per second. The larger the baud rate, the faster information will be transmitted.
browser	A browser is a software program that allows one to navigate the Internet. Normally browsers are associated with navigation of the World Wide Web. The advantage of browsers is their ability to assume a great deal of the work involved in moving around the Internet. Some popular WWW browsers include Netscape Navigator, Mosaic, Internet in a Box, and Emissary.
distribution list	A group of e-mail addresses that can automatically be inserted into an e-mail message to allow the user to send the same message to multiple addresses.
domain name	The domain name is part of your e-mail address. It represents the service provider, the computer you access from your service provider (if they have more than one), and a suffix that identifies the provider as being a commercial, educational, or governmental site.
e-mail	(Electronic Mail) A method of sending and receiving text messages via computer rather than traditional surface mail.
FAQ	(Frequently Asked Questions) FAQs are postings that attempt to address frequently asked questions by users in an effort to provide assistance. These postings or messages reduce the amount of individual requests for assistance.
filtering	Automatic sorting of incoming e-mail messages according to the sender, words contained in the message, or the message topic.
flaming	Abusive or inflammatory language in posting an electronic message.
ftp	(File Transfer Protocol) This is the computer language that allows you to receive software programs or files on the Internet.
home page	Pages or screens on the World Wide Web.
hypertext	A nonsequential computer software tool that links various sources of information together, allowing the user to move or jump to any location at will. Normally the user clicks the mouse on text or an icon that links the user to text, graphic, video, or audio information.
Internet service providers	These are private and public entities that provide the connection to the backbone of the Internet. Examples of service providers are large commercial companies such as CompuServe and America Online, public institutions such as universities, and smaller commercial operations that limit their service to local or regional areas.

IRC	(Internet Relay Chat) IRCs allow Internet users to chat, or type on screen, as others view that message in real time from distant locations. Similar to talking on the phone, except the communication is one screen in text.
ISDN	(Integrated Service Digital Network) These are relatively new forms of communicating on the Internet. ISDN lines allow one to simultaneously use the line for both digital and analog service; thus one can talk on the phone and be connected to the Internet at the same time.
Kbps	(kilobits per second) A kilobit is 1,000 bits of information where a bit is 1 character of information. The kilobit is used to define how much information can be carried across phone or fiber lines per second. Thus a modem operating at 14.4 Kbps transfers 14,400 bits of information per second.
LAN	(Local Area Network) Numerous computers that are linked or can communicate with each other directly on a network that is relatively small. Typically a LAN is established within a building or a department within a building.
listserv	An automated system that distributes e-mail to individuals. To obtain e-mail from a specific listserv, a user must first subscribe to the listserv group.
login	Also referred to as logging in to the computer. This is the process of establishing a connection to your host computer or service provider and normally requires entering a user name and password.
Mbps	(megabits per second) A megabit is 1,000,000 bits of information. A bit is a character, the smallest unit of information used by a computer. The megabit is used to define how much information can be carried across phone or fiber lines per second. Thus a direct connection to the Internet, such as a T1 line, can carry 1.544 Mbps or 1,544,000,000 bits per second! Compare that to 14,400 bits per second carried by a 14.4 baud modem.
netiquette	This is the desired behavior that one assumes as he or she is on the Internet. Common forms of netiquette require, for example, that one not post the same message on numerous newsgroups, make use of inappropriate language, or send inane messages on e-mail.
newbies	Individuals who are new to the Internet and its use.
newsgroups	This is a message area on the Internet that is dedicated to a specific topic or body of interest. Users of newsgroups can post messages, reply to posted messages, and send e-mail directly to a member of the newsgroup.
offline mailers	Mail programs that allow you to compose a message even though you are not connected to the Internet. Once you connect to the Net, the program allows you to send or receive messages. Normally offline mail programs, such as Eudora, reside on your computer.
online mailers	Mail programs that allow you to compose within the mail program only once you are connected. Normally online mail programs (such as PINE) reside on your service provider's computer.
PPP	(Point-to-Point Protocol) This is one of the two commonly used standard languages used to connect to the Internet via telephone lines.

search engines	Programs on the World Wide Web that search the Web for information, people, software, etc.
SGML	(Standard Generalized Markup Language) A language used to create programs on the WWW that determine how text and graphics will appear.
SHOUTING	This is a term to describe the messages of users who use ALL CAPITAL LETTERS in their messages.
SLIP	(Serial Line Internet Protocol) This is a protocol or standard language that allows one to connect to the Internet via a phone line.
spamming	The process of bombarding an individual with e-mail in response to some form of offensive behavior. Spamming is a popular response to individuals who post unwanted advertisements on multiple newsgroups.
URL	(Uniform Resource Locator) The Internet address for sites on the World Wide Web. Each site has its own distinct address.
Usenet	A group of systems that exchange information in the form of newsgroups across the Internet.
video conferencing	Live or almost live video broadcasting from one location to another using the Internet to transport the visual image.
VRML	(Virtual Reality Modeling Language) A computer software language that allows one to program in a virtual reality environment where the screen gives the illusion of being in a three-dimensional world.
WAN	(Wide Area Network) Numerous computers that are linked together by a network that extends over a large geographic area.
WWW	(World Wide Web) A huge global network of linked computer sites that point to or direct the user to text, graphic, sound, and video information. A unique element of the Web is the navigational process of hypertext, allowing the user to simply click on text that then links the user to various global sites.

Index